FIRE IN THE HOLE

One Man's Journey Through the Trauma of PTSD

To Deirdre,
+ in peace and
best wishes in your
life + work —
Bill

★ ★ ★ ★ ★ ★

WILLIAM LARSEN

Copyright

Dedication

*This book is dedicated to the casualties of all wars,
victims and perpetrators alike.*

Table of Contents

...War's a game, which,
were their subjects wise,
Kings would not play...

— *William Cowper*

PROLOGUE

Throughout history the human species has fought innumerable wars inflicting calculable injury, death, and loss on those exposed to combat. There is also a darker, more pervasive—and far less calculable—underside of war, and that is the ongoing psychological damage suffered by victims (and sometimes perpetrators) long after the traumatic events have passed. This is a disease known as post-traumatic stress disorder (PTSD).

In the past, several terms were used to label the emotional affliction manifested by combat veterans, including "shell shock," "battle fatigue," "war neurosis," and "combat stress reaction." Long before this phenomenon was clinically understood, the reality of postwar trauma had been documented in literary and historical works, such as Homer's *The Iliad*, Shakespeare's *Henry IV*, and Dickens' *A Tale of Two Cities*. Such works and terms acknowledge the existence of post-war psychological trauma but do little to identify its underlying cause.

Modern medical science now understands the etiology of PTSD, noting that when under severe trauma, the body's sympathetic nervous system generates stress hormones (e.g., cortisol and epinephrine) to stimulate the energy needed to negotiate the life-threatening situation. The survival mechanism known as the "fight, flight, or freeze" syndrome is triggered, providing limited options for the individual's response. Under most circumstances, this hyperarousal peaks during the trauma and effectively drains from the body afterward, reestablishing balance. While the behaviors needed for trauma response may be highly functional in the moment, if the hyperarousal persists, destructive patterns often develop that create dysfunction in the individual's life.

Ongoing pathology occurs when such devastating memories are stitched so deeply into the nervous system that they create a catastrophic lens of terror and rage through which the individual views even harmless situations. This hyperarousal leads to ongoing rounds of emotional and behavioral overreaction, social avoidance, and acting out that create severe dysfunction, damaging the individual's personal relationships and emotional well-being. It has been estimated that thirty percent of Vietnam vets experienced PTSD at some point in their lives and that 271,000 still suffer from some level of the disorder. After many years of neglect, the Veterans Administration has been active in identifying the presence of this disorder and providing therapy and drug medication to the afflicted individuals.

PTSD is not limited to war, of course, and the disorder occurs in individuals suffering abnormal life-threatening situations like rape, physical assault, natural disaster, witnessing horrific violence perpetrated on others, etc. In the late '70s, it was the combination of studies on both rape and combat survivors that spurred the psychiatric profession to classify PTSD as a distinct disorder. It is the prevalence of PTSD among combat veterans, however, that is the concern of this book as well as the journey related herein.

The decision to title this book *Fire in the Hole* stems from its double meaning. While the expression is military slang for an impending explosion in a confined space, it specifically relates to the warning called out by soldiers when throwing tear gas grenades into bunkers to contaminate the enemy's abode. The term is also an apt metaphor for the phenomenon of PTSD itself. The emotional suffering experienced by many survivors of violent trauma may be seen as a "hot grenade" creating intense inner fire that often explodes into rage or other disruptive behavior. PTSD plagues the lives of millions throughout the world, and increased research on effective treatments is clearly needed. In effect, those suffering the lingering effects of horrific trauma are experiencing "fire in the hole" in their very being.

PREFACE

I never planned to go back to Nam. And I sure as hell didn't plan to go there in the first place. But in my life, Vietnam doesn't work that way. Forces beyond my control seemed to be guiding my return in 1996, much as they had in 1969. In both cases the journeys were as unexpected as they were necessary.

In 1996 I'd been working as a contract psychotherapist with the Veterans Administration for eight years, treating combat veterans whose issues were much the same as my own. Twenty-seven years earlier, I'd served with an infantry company in the Vietnamese jungle near Cambodia. In my ten weeks there, our company lost nearly forty percent of its numbers—dead or wounded. I was the only medic. Three AK-47 rounds cut that trip mercifully short, but a ten-month hospitalization did nothing to ease the pain of my own wounding and the memory of seeing so many young men exploded into human mush. Consequently, after my discharge from the Army hospital at Fort Riley, Kansas, my life tumbled into a downward spiral that nearly got me nabbed in a Mexican heroin bust.

And *that* was the eye-opener that convinced me to get help.

Years of psychological treatment led to graduate school and eventually to state licensure as a psychotherapist. Through the mid-'70s I worked at a clinic, saw private clients, and taught part time at the university where I'd earned my master's degree. Life was good again, and it got a whole lot better when I met my soulmate, Barbara. We married in 1977, and a year later, sick of the Bay Area congestion, we moved to a small Northern California town in the Sierra Nevada to start a family and open a private practice.

We immediately took to small-town life. I began seeing private clients, and Barbara used her master's degree in special education to work with developmentally disabled adults. We built our house on three acres of land a few miles outside of town and settled in, anticipating our future children.

Tragically, our first baby died in a botched home birth performed by an incompetent midwife. The loss of our son was harder to deal with than anything I'd experienced in Vietnam, and it triggered my PTSD big time. Our marriage survived through the power of prayer, meditation, and therapy, and three and a half years later our beloved daughter Claire was born. Her name, derived from Latin, roughly translates to "clear light," and that's truly what she brought to our lives.

It all seemed so hopeful then. Our little homestead in the woods was an idyllic setting, and I felt fortunate beyond belief to have survived to this point, let alone to be blessed with a loving family. I wanted nothing more than to be with my baby, so I was largely a stay-at-home dad during the first few years of Claire's life. I reveled in our forest romps and in-town adventures as she developed into a little girl. Life was more than good again; it was everything I had dreamed it could be.

Unfortunately, the bottom was about to fall out.

Reopening my practice, I began seeing private clients, worked in the county's sexual-abuse program, and organized a therapy group for combat veterans. After wrestling so long with my own demons, treating the traumas of others was the last thing I would have expected, but the recognition of PTSD (post-traumatic stress disorder) in 1980 caused a nationwide flood of veterans seeking psychological treatment. A system of vet centers was established in urban communities, and contracts were offered in remote areas to enable rural veterans to receive ongoing treatment without having to travel long distances to get it. In 1988 I received one of those contracts.

The program took off immediately; my phone started ringing the day after the contract was signed. The calls were largely from combat vets, and their stories were all variations of the experiences I had undergone. Initially, taking in so many gruesome stories seemed under control, and my work and family life remained reasonably separate. Before long, however, the vets' stories began spinning and looping in my mind, making it harder to leave them at the office door, harder to soften back into the needs of a young family after steeling myself to get through the day.

Increasingly, I'd startle awake in the middle of the night, my body humming like a high-voltage wire from the traumatic overload. I'd thrash about for hours, finding sleep impossible due to the adrenaline firing my nervous system as I anticipated a full slate of vets the next day. When sleep did come, I sometimes had nightmares about combat stories related by vets earlier in the day.

As the years passed, I settled into the pattern I'd mastered in Vietnam—repress feelings, suck in my gut, and keep going regardless of the cost.

Eventually I hired a subcontractor to help with my caseload, and when her schedule quickly filled, I hired another. The stress went on for years, and little by little I began withdrawing into a cocoon of grim, tight-lipped endurance that was shutting out those I loved most. For the first five years of Claire's life, I had been a devoted dad, with an ever-available lap that was a safe port for the little girl whose light had opened my heart. But then, like a slow-growing cancer, my life devolved into a pattern of work, isolation, monster mood swings, and an increasing reliance on alcohol to dull the pain. There was never physical abuse, but the former safe port had become a mined harbor as the father Claire trusted and loved turned into a snarling recluse, storming around the house like a man chased by vengeful ghosts.

By the time 1996 rolled around, I had alienated my wife and daughter so much that they were planning a trip to visit Barbara's relatives in Italy—without me. And I was trying to understand why I didn't care. I was caught in a trap of my own making, and I had no idea what to do about it. Once again, however, as they had in the past, those forces beyond my control intervened to offer a way forward.

In November of 1995 I was shopping at our local grocery store and was handed a five-dollar bill as change. On impulse, I plopped the bill into a lottery machine and pocketed the ticket. When I scratched it off later that evening, I was astounded to see that I had won $10,000. I used part of the money to pay for Barbara and Claire's trip to Italy, but I wasn't sure what to do with the rest of my winnings. Although the financial windfall was greatly appreciated, it did nothing to resolve our family crisis. It was a dark time—and getting darker—when a glimmer of light illuminated a path.

In the mid-1990s Bill Clinton had lifted the trade embargo on our old enemy, and the news media began crackling with stories of a "new Vietnam." Our former nemesis, the reports said, had become a land of civil reform and rising economic opportunity. Its people had overcome the shackles of the past and were embracing a future based on prosperity and peace rather than on armed conflict. Caught up in the multifaceted crisis of my life, this message of hope was just what I needed to hear. Perhaps, I thought, if I witnessed Vietnam's recovery, I just might foster my own. So, bowing to my good fortune—whether it be pure luck or divine intervention—I decided to see for myself.

This is the story of that journey.

CH 1
JUNE 2, 1969–*Long Binh*

I was lying in a hospital bed in Long Binh, jaws wired, tracheotomy, tubes strung like guy-wires into my nose, throat, chest, and both arms. Earlier in the month, the Army brass had flown my company deep into the jungle near Cambodia, landing us in a field next to an enemy bunker complex. Piling out of the choppers, we swarmed into the rainforest and set up our perimeter. A patrol sent out to locate the North Vietnamese bunkers was met by an avalanche of enemy fire. Several of the grunts got hit, and if Nam taught me any one thing it's this: when grunts get hit, there's one word that rips from their lips right along with *aaagh*, *please God*, and *motherfucker*—and that word is *medic*.

I'd heard it before. Heard it way too often. Heard it and responded as my hard-ass, blue-collar father taught me—headfirst into the fight. For some time that strategy had worked. I waded through the ruptured guts of others and came out clean. This time was different. This time I got hit as I crawled into a clearing to reach two grunts who had gotten ambushed by the North Vietnamese Army (NVA). I took a sniper round flush on the chin that shattered my jaw. One minute I was firing my M-16 into the jungle, applying a little preventive medicine, the next I was part of a three-man heap.

Out cold. Then bubbles, hearing bubbles, breathing bubbles. Choking!

Face down in a pool of blood, I woke up gagging on the syrupy fluid getting sucked into my nose and throat. From then on it was twilight time, coming in and out of consciousness, voices yelling, "Medic hit! Medic hit!," bursts of NVA rifle rounds kicking up dirt behind us, our troops firing back, U.S. artillery shells blasting the jungle where the enemy was dug in. Shards of jawbone were hanging off my chin, and I couldn't see a thing because of the blood soaking my face. *Dear Jesus*, I remember thinking, *how did I get myself into this?*

CH 2
FEBRUARY 28, 1996–*Nevada City, California*

It was a glorious day in the foothills, with a sweet bite to the air as the sodden hillsides rose green and wet from the winter sludge. Stretching into the warmest breeze in months, I let the sun's buttery fingers ooze like oil into my winter skin. For several days the forested slopes of the western Sierra had been drenched in a frigid downpour, then sharp as a rifle crack, the weather bolted hot and dry. One day, mud soup. The next, a sudden gush of florid warmth.

I was sitting on my slate patio beneath a cluster of oaks, watching our dog Lilly scatter squirrels around the manzanita-dotted hillside. At my feet the rounded edge of a small ornamental pool rose into a three-tiered waterfall that bathed me in its velvety murmur. Anchored elbow to knee on a redwood bench, I couldn't help chuckling at my pup's frantic, if fruitless, pursuit through the towering ponderosa pines. I hoped she wouldn't ruin the game by catching one of the furry critters, who were the source of both her frustration and her delight.

I'd settled on the bench a bit earlier, watching the goldfish hovering around the large rocks I had dropped in that year. Predators had been a major cause of goldfish depletion since I sank the pool, and I often found myself on that bench, usually at dusk, marveling at how the fish went for cover as night started creeping in. But it was only 4 p.m., so I figured they were traumatized by the liquid strafing Lilly's exuberance produced and needed to stay near their little bunkers.

I could definitely relate.

Most definitely, for even as I reveled in the momentary joy, my gut was screwed tight as a coffin lid. Every few moments my gaze shifted from the tranquil pond to my blue pickup truck parked in the driveway. The green camo backpack framed in its side window told me all I needed to know about the coming days, and seeing it there, all I could do was shake my head, peer deeper into the water, and realize as if for the first time, *Holy shit, it's really happening. I'm going back to Nam.*

The water was a bit murky from the splashing, but I could see my reflection on the pool's sunlit surface: a small man, slightly stooped, balding but well fringed, with wire-rimmed spectacles crookedly aligned over a scraggly, gray-flecked beard. Dressed in a tan, four-pocketed traveling jacket, he sat still as a rock, only his fingers moving, twisting a blue and white baseball cap with the words *Free Tibet* printed in bold red letters across the front. The contours of his face were blurred, but I could see the eyes locked like radar on the rustling wet screen, as if trying to freeze the image wavering in and out of focus.

But there was no stopping, no final form. The swirling image seemed to mock that very notion, and caught within a slough of old memories and present regrets, I could only wonder at how disjointed my life had become over the last several years. A confusing array of sensations flooded me at that moment. Beyond all else, even in the midst of our family crisis, it felt so good to bask in the warmth, safely ensconced on the patch of land I had homesteaded with my wife and daughter eleven years earlier. It was the only home my adult life had known. But this burst of tranquility was muted by a sense of deep apprehension.

I didn't know what I'd find in the Vietnam of 1996, but I sure remembered the chaotic, blood-crazed inferno of 1969. As I pondered the journey, images from the war were lighting up my mind like rocket fire, conjuring scenes of slaughter and loss and wounds that never heal. As clearly as I knew those events were in the distant past, the years of being inundated by the stories of the vets I'd treated made it feel like I was still there. No matter how hard I tried, it was impossible to separate the Vietnam I had known from the foreign country I'd soon be visiting.

One thing was for sure: this was no pleasure trip I was about to undertake, no tropical South Sea holiday. My life was already plenty difficult, and a solo trip into the land of my worst nightmares felt as alluring as a bout of intestinal surgery. The thought of going back to Vietnam had never occurred to me until recently, and what I hoped to gain from my return was no clearer than the face wavering in and out of focus on the pond's shimmery surface.

CH 3
1956–*Omaha, Nebraska*

Even before going to Vietnam the first time, I was never quite clear whose face that was staring back at me. The issue had to do with how I was raised.

We were a working-class Catholic family, rooted squarely and solidly in conservative Midwestern values, as well plotted in our ways as the checkerboard farmlands surrounding Omaha, Nebraska. My entire life had been spent within the narrow confines of a small Catholic parish, home of the Redemptorist fathers and Servants of Mary nuns. Like my older brothers, I attended the parish's K-12 school, served the priests as an altar boy at Mass, and played on school teams. After high school, I enrolled at nearby O.U. (Omaha University), paying for my education by working summer construction jobs. It was textbook parochial. My friends from high school were my friends in college; our families had known one another forever. Some of our older siblings had even married one another.

I was the youngest of five, following two sisters and two brothers on a street ironically named 'Military Avenue'. Our father was a self-employed plasterer, a one-man operation patching older buildings constructed before the advent of sheetrock, which came along after World War II and turned plastering into a dying art.

Although she does not figure predominantly in my war story, my mother was the backbone of our family, working a full time job to supplement my dad's dwindling wages and tending to her family at night. Denied accepting a full-ride scholarship after high school because of the Great Depression, she began taking college classes in her mid-50's and earned a Master's Degree in Occupational Therapy. I could write a book about this remarkable woman, but that's a different story, and the parent whose influence led me to the battlefield was my father.

Earnest Hulbert Larsen was, emphatically, a Dane as well as a plasterer, plying the trade that had been brought over from the old country by his grandfather, Ernst Larsen. He was a rough, loving, sports-obsessed Viking enthusiast who started his boys mixing mortar at an early age. This was a matter of family economics as well as of filial responsibility. When his wages became inadequate to support the family, he saved money by conscripting his three sons as laborers. Consequently, from our twelfth year on, we relinquished our summers to "tend" him as he tore off old plaster and troweled in the new, while we mixed and hauled the heavy "mud" up endless flights of stairs.

The Old Man was a hard boss, but a fair one. He was a screamer who stood for no slacking off on the job, but he could be mellow when things were going well and we had to wait for the first coat of plaster to set. It was tough love for sure, but he had a flair for mixing affection with outrage, and although I hated the discipline, there were many good times talking about sports and life and hearing stories of his childhood and parents, who had died before I was born. I can still see him dressed in his white overalls, smoking a cigar and laughing as he reminisced about the past. Then the break was over and *nobody* laughed until the job was done.

Much later, with the advent of the men's movement, it was odd to hear how many modern sons never really knew their fathers, who worked outside the home. It sure wasn't that way with us. I could love him or I could hate him, but one thing was never in doubt: I *knew* my dad.

The Old Man's passion for sports was paramount in his parenting. This put me in a tough position because, alone among my brothers, I took after my maternal grandfather, a small, slightly built fellow who played the clarinet and had absolutely no aptitude for combative athletics. I never doubted my father's love, and when I proved I could do the same work he demanded from my older brothers, there was a look of satisfaction in his eyes that made the verbal abuse almost tolerable. But the fact was, with the build of a spaghetti noodle and a dreamy, introverted disposition that kept my head floating in the clouds, I was never able to succeed on the field of dreams that so captivated my dad's attention. As non-lethal as it may seem, that failure created an identity crisis only another boy noodle could understand.

My father, who loved me dearly, tried to hide his disappointment in his thin, awkward son. The fact was, however, given our differences in physiology and temperament, the avenues for pleasing him were limited.

But there was one.

This I discovered as a little boy sitting on his lap in The Assembly, one of the three neighborhood bars that dotted Military Avenue. The *Catholic* tavern. It was at The Assembly where, on Saturday afternoons, men from our local parish gathered to watch sports programs, argue politics, drink beer, and, above all, tell stories. Along with a few other kids, I would sit with them, slurping soda pop and listening as the men unwound from the week. My dad, who could be as physically affectionate as he was heavy-handed, often held me on his lap as he joined in the good-hearted bantering.

During these discussions, my father basked like a proud stag among his peers, secure in the world he knew and those with whom he shared it. His hands were happy and alive, squishing me in their massive warm grip as he hooted and hawed, reveling in the animated camaraderie of The Assembly. But then, as often happened, one subject emerged and the dancing hands froze.

World War II. My father's albatross.

The short story was, he didn't go. There were lots of reasons, three in fact, then a fourth when brother Steve was born in 1943. What was the man to do? Since high school, where he was an all-state athlete in two sports, he had been one of the baddest guys on the street, a Viking Adonis who had the admiration of all the women and could look any man straight in the eye. When the Big

One came along, it was only natural that he would extend his warrior's quest onto the killing fields of combat. Yet he did not. Our dad *wanted* to go, we were told, but gave in to Mother's adamant assertion that parental responsibility far outweighed the paltry contribution one more father of four could have on the war's outcome.

So my father participated in the war as a civilian, taking the observer's stance he would later be thrust into at The Assembly. He contributed in his own way, lending his craft to local organizations supporting the war effort, but none of his children remember him ever mentioning his work repairing masonry disasters at the old Fort Omaha Army station.

On those Saturday afternoons, tucked into my dad's arms, I couldn't help but notice how the energy in the room changed when war became the topic. How the tones softened, the words slowed. How the men shifted uneasily in their chairs (some far more uneasy than others). Understanding little, I saw how the ranking in the room turned in these moments, taking on a life that would exist only as long as the subject was pursued, the stories told. They were war-tellers, these men—*wah-tellas* I called them in my little boy's voice. And everyone laughed.

But when a *wah-tella* spoke, the other men listened. As *I* listened, caught in open-mouthed awe at thunderously explosive scenes where men were killed and maimed, saved or lost, proven or permanently disgraced. The stories helped explain the great mystery of my childhood: the call to be a man. How wonderful, I thought, that there was a test to resolve this mystery. That there could be proof.

As thrilling as they were, the *wah-tellas'* words burned less deeply in my consciousness than my father's gnarled hands did as they tightened around my belly. Tightening as he and the other nonveterans were reduced to the quiet attention of spectators. Having never fought on that ultimate field, the Old Man carried a pained deference toward those who had. And even then, perched on his suddenly stiffened lap, I knew the fingers clenched in shame, that those who were not *wah-tellas* felt themselves somehow less than these tellers of war. Less as men.

In this way, a new branch grew on our family tree, and although that memory receded as I grew, a root was planted that later determined my relationship with Vietnam. I would fight the war my father had failed to fight, pass the test for both of us so the beloved fingers would never again writhe in the wake of other men's words.

And my own doubt could be put to rest.

CH 4
MARCH 12, 1969-*Viet Nam*

Following a couple of detours that will be explained shortly, I was inducted into the U.S. Army on August 25, 1968, and sent for basic training to Fort Lewis, Washington. Basic was essentially an exercise in taking orders and undergoing the humiliation of being herded like sheep through a series of classes and field maneuvers, marching in formation, and engaging in physical exercises and work details. We also had to qualify on using the M-16 rifle.

After basic, I was sent to Fort Sam Houston in San Antonio for AIT (advanced individual training). Fort Sam was the home of the Army's medical corps, and for reasons never clear to me, I had been ordered to undergo a ten-week training course as a medic. This training turned out to be of limited use, since it was totally generic and geared for medics in *all* settings: triage, hospitals, clinics, etc. The part focusing on what combat medics needed to know was so meager it could have been done in a long weekend.

After the training, I was given a one-month home leave with orders to report afterward to Travis Air Force Base in California. At that point it was transport to Vietnam. But it was a joy to escape the Army's clutches for a while, and I spent the time hanging out with family and friends, helping the Old Man on his plaster jobs and otherwise doing as little as possible. Most of my old group were either married or had moved out of Omaha, but I did connect with a couple of guys and spent a few nights a week playing poker and hanging out in the neighborhood tavern—smoking, getting shit-faced, playing endless games of shuffleboard, and wondering why we didn't have dates. I don't know about my buddies, but for my part I had a good reason for staying away from the local women.

During my medic training and while I was on leave, I exchanged phone calls with a young woman I'd met in the Extension Volunteers. Charlene was from Colorado, and had visited my family the previous Christmas. I convinced myself that I was in love, but that was at least partly due to the fact that I was headed for a war zone, and needed a sweetheart waiting for me while I was away. After much pressuring on my part, she agreed that we would marry a few months after I returned.

The days turned to weeks, and the weeks started rolling by. I attended Mass on Sundays, and sometimes a weekday morning service, as well. As my reporting date neared, I also found myself drawn to Friday evening vespers. There was an ancient liturgy behind the ritual, but for me it was more visceral than sacramental: the shadowy quiet of our near-empty church, fumes of pungent incense spicing the shrouded darkness, the droning Latin incantations of the priest offering his small congregation to God at the end of day. Knowing I was heading into a life-threatening situation undoubtedly triggered my need for divine solace. All I know is that I found deep comfort in giving myself up to a power greater than myself.

I did make one effort to find spiritual guidance from a more human source. A week before leaving, I approached the rectory of a neighboring parish and asked to speak to the residing priest (the ones in my parish were unavailable because of an ecclesiastical conference). An elderly, haggard-looking housekeeper answered the door and sat me in the waiting room as she left to fetch the "good Father." After twenty minutes or so, a corpulent middle-aged man came trudging down the wooden staircase, snorting loudly as he buckled his pants and tucked in a white undershirt. It was clear that he had been napping and was not happy for the interruption.

He was nearly monosyllabic in his dismissive platitudes and clearly had little interest in my predicament. Seeing he had nothing to offer, I quickly cut the visit short. He did not offer a priestly blessing as I rose to leave.

This encounter, along with several others in the military, pretty much eroded my trust in authority. What I never did lose, however, was my love for the sweet sanctuary of vespers and the immense relief of surrendering to a higher power.

The day before I left for Vietnam, my parents and I went to a movie, then Mom fried up a huge rib steak so I had one good meal before going back to Army chow. The next morning, we rose early so they could get me to the airport for the flight to San Francisco. We parted with hugs and sad eyes, but no tears. I pretty much dozed in my window seat until the captain announced we were starting our descent.

After landing in San Francisco, the airport intercom directed me to a room for incoming military personnel. There I joined a few dozen other GIs, and we were soon loaded onto a bus taking us to Travis. Upon arriving at the airbase, we were dropped off at a huge warehouse where we joined a few hundred other guys—and a small number of women—waiting for their departure call. We were all issued green jungle fatigues, and that was the last time in months that I saw anyone dressed in anything else.

The warehouse was home for the next few days, and people came and went in droves. When my name was finally called, I joined a group of several dozen others, then underwent three separate roll calls before being led to the tarmac and boarding the plane. Trudging up the ramp, I had a sickening premonition that once we were airborne, my life would never be the same.

By 1969, the military was shipping replacements on civilian flights, and the only two things I remember were the female flight attendants and the fact that, when we had a layover in Hawaii, none of the airport bars was open. It was a lengthy layover, and we passed time by walking around, reading, and playing cards. We had been expressly forbidden to drink alcohol by the sergeant escorting us, but that wouldn't have stopped several of us from imbibing. We had more to worry about than military discipline, and were already adopting the fuck-the-Army attitude so common among grunts in

Vietnam. As the saying went if you got caught bucking authority, "What are you going to do, send me to Nam?"

Back on the plane, we lifted off for Asia, and several hours later (after landing in Guam for refueling), we descended into the Tan Son Nhut Air Base near Saigon. It was a couple of hours before dawn, around 9:00 p.m. in California, and the apprehensive looks on the faces of the stewardesses reminded us that we were flying into a war zone.

My first impression of Vietnam was the blast of fiery air when the cabin door was opened, and I had the ominous realization that it was still dark outside and likely the coolest time of day. I'd known high temperatures in Nebraska, but Asian heat turned out to be of a different order entirely. Fortunately, I had no idea then how magnified the heat became when humping seventy-five-pound rucksacks through the steaming jungle.

We exited the plane and were marched into a huge lit-up tent for processing. Groggy and jet-lagged, our mood wasn't helped by being called newbies or FNGs (fucking new guys) by the personnel checking us in. I don't remember much else about that grand entry, just a lot of roll calls and waiting until we were mercifully taken to a barracks and allowed to lay it down.

Because we didn't get to bed until around 5:00 a.m., our little group was allowed to sleep late. We had chow, and then stood in formation where we were told that we'd be there for a few days to acclimatize to the weather and wait for our duty assignments. My memory is pretty blurred on those first few days, but I remember we were given orientation briefings and put on work details to clean the barracks, haul trash, and pick up cigarette butts. We were still pretty wasted from jet-lag, heat reactions, and the stark realization of where we were, so unlike most times in the military, not that much was asked of us for the first few days.

Most of the GIs were bound for the infantry or its supportive services—artillery, sniper training, demolition—but a few lucky ones would be assigned as clerks, hospital orderlies, chaplain assistants, or some other enviable rear job. The odds of that were poor, but chance was the ruling factor, even then. Several days later, I was told I'd been assigned to the 1st Air Cavalry Division. FNG that I was, my orders stated that I'd be flown north to the An Khe Army base for further orientation and jungle warfare training.

My memory about that training is also sketchy, but I do remember a make-shift Vietnamese hamlet composed of several hootches with thatched roofs. We were also shown a punji pit with razor-sharp stakes at the bottom of a camouflaged hole.

"They smear shit on the stakes," the training sergeant told us, "and if you step into one of those fuckers, you got an infection that'll take you out quick as an AK-47 round. All I can say, gentlemen, is watch your step."

It was at An Khe where I experienced my first mortar attack. The rounds came in with no warning one night, landing fairly close to our Quonset hut. We were immediately hustled into an underground bunker as explosions thundered above us.

"Welcome to Vietnam," our trainer called out to us as we sat wide-eyed and scared on the rough wooden benches. "Y'all get this in the boonies, drop on your belly and find a big tree." He paused, as if scanning through his memories. "Good luck on that." Later, we heard that the mortar rounds had torn up a bit of the airstrip, but no injuries were reported.

At An Khe, we also had to re-qualify with the M-16 rifle on the firing range. Accuracy was never my thing, and I remember one grizzled old NCO telling us to not worry if we couldn't hit the target, because in the jungle, there was rarely anybody to shoot at anyway.

"Just hot shit pouring outta the bush," he said. "Charlie sees you, but you don't see him, got it?"

He paused for a moment to let that sink in.

"That's pretty much it, newbies. Just be sure yer pointin' yer weapon in the right direction, then let 'er rip on full auto. Do that, keep yer head down, and wait for the artillery. It'll do the dirty work."

Our M-16s were usually set on semi-automatic, firing one round at a time, but could be flipped to full auto to lay out twenty rounds in two-and-a-half seconds. The enemy, we were told, used AK-47s that held thirty-round magazines and were considered to be a superior weapon because of the M-16's tendency to jam. Heads snapped up around the room when we heard that.

I finished the training and was assigned to my new unit: D Company, 1st Battalion, 5th Cavalry, 1st Cavalry Division—or more simply, Delta 1/5. The next day, I was flown south to the Tay Ninh Army base where I reported to the battalion medical corps and waited for the order to join D Company in "the field"—a term that referred to the vast jungle between Vietnam and Cambodia. This area was euphemistically dubbed a free-fire zone or no man's land, because all the indigenous people had been forcibly relocated from their hamlets to the Tay Ninh Army base. Since those who were left were considered to be enemy combatants, our mission was to attack anyone we found.

The order soon came, and one afternoon I boarded a Huey helicopter to join my new unit. This chopper was sent out every few days to resupply the company with its basic needs: ammo, C-rations, water, beer, field dressings and...medics.

The chopper soared hundreds of feet above the deceptively gorgeous jungle, a vibrantly green canvas with a few silvery rivers snaking through the emerald forest. I soon learned, however, that viewing it from the air could not have been more different from traipsing through that same jungle beneath its stifling, prickly, insect-infested canopy.

Within a half-hour, we landed in a large field of elephant grass, and the supplies were unloaded by several grunts who took me to meet the company's commanding officer, Captain Pat Bates. He welcomed me to the unit and told me I was officially on loan to the company from the battalion medical corps. He explained that I would be responsible for monitoring medical supplies, distributing anti-malaria tablets, and putting in requests for needed items through his nightly radio contact with battalion headquarters.

I was then introduced to the only other medic, a skinny Black guy who wouldn't look me in the eye and answered my questions with grunting monosyllables before leaving abruptly to rejoin his buddies. Later, I learned that the Black men in the company largely kept to themselves and wanted as little contact as possible with their white comrades, a situation all too common at that racially charged time.

My division was air mobile, meaning we had Huey helicopters to fly us in and out of hot spots as the brass saw fit. Our company was one of four assigned to guard LZ (landing zone) Dolly, a hilltop encampment the size of a football field on top of an Agent Orange-denuded hill. Such landing zones were scattered throughout the jungle to establish an American force in our fight against the North Vietnamese Army (NVA). They were all composed of a landing zone for helicopters, artillery guns, and an intelligence post with advanced radio capacity to intercept enemy communications and transmit such information to our superiors in the rear (colloquially called "REMFS" or "rear echelon motherfuckers"). Dolly was protected by a series of elevated bunkers strategically set around the hill's perimeter that were manned by the various companies in the battalion.

Our current mission, I was told, was to intercept NVA troops retreating from their assaults on various cities in the second Tet Offensive, and take whatever prisoners we could. Capturing prisoners was actually a top priority, because they were a prime source of intelligence, and, once thoroughly interrogated might be turned into *chieu-hois*—the term for enemy soldiers who came over to our side as Kit Carson scouts to help our forces navigate the jungle and understand how the NVA operated. The battalion's COs actually had contests to see which company could provide the brass with the most candidates for the *chieu-hoi* program.

For three weeks a month, each company wandered the forest floor, seeking out enemy forces and attacking the large NVA bunker complexes scattered throughout the jungle. The company was then rotated to LZ Dolly to man the perimeter and guard the outpost.

I was assigned to one of the company's platoons (approximately thirty men, three platoons to a company), and a couple of the grunts filled me in on what to expect in the days ahead. The routine was pretty simple. Every day, we "humped" several kilometers on a route provided by the battalion commander seeking NVA troops to engage. The company then set up camp, sending a few men outside the perimeter as forward observation posts to guard against enemy assaults.

The exception to this routine occurred when an NVA bunker complex was discovered, and we were flown in to check it out. These complexes were massive earthen structures built out of logs and sand bags, then covered with brush, to house the enemy as they coordinated assaults against our forces. Woven intricately into the wiry jungle, they were virtually invisible from the air, but were spotted when a recon plane observed soldiers moving about the area. One of the battalion's companies was then sent to investigate.

As it happened, that's exactly what was planned the next morning.

I settled in with my new comrades and was shown the nightly ritual. Setting up our camp was no easy task, because it involved constructing our own bunkers. This we did by digging trenches five feet deep and six feet long, stacking two sand bags at each end of the trench. Cutting several small trees, we propped them on the end bags and laid them over the hole, filling more sand bags to cover the logs, which completed our makeshift roof. These bunkers were spaced evenly around the perimeter, with four to six grunts assigned to each one, ready to dive into them if attacked.

Later that afternoon as the sun was lowering, we began cooking our individual dinners using small chunks of the malleable clay-like C-4 explosive to heat our food. I had never heard of C-4, but learned that a thumb-sized chunk of the stuff could be lit to provide a small fire, while several bars wrapped in an electrical wire set off a thunderous explosion when detonated. Doing so triggered an avalanche of deadly shrapnel that ripped bodies to shreds. I was amazed at how well the C-4 worked, and heated a meal of tasteless canned food ("C-rats") that went down like coagulated mud. After eating, we cleaned our utensils, and since it was getting dark, we started claiming our individual sleeping spots around the bunker, padding the ground with brush to create an illusion of comfort.

That night, I got my first taste of sleeping on the heavily matted forest floor. Wrapped in my green poncho liner, I couldn't help thinking about my friends in the Extension Volunteers, wondering where I'd be now if the dice had rolled differently. I yearned for sleep, but lay awake for hours pondering what the next day would bring. The NVA bunker complex we were being flown to was battalion-sized, my platoon commander had said, meaning far bigger than most and probably more fiercely defended.

"Get ready for a hot LZ, doc," he muttered. "Gooks'll probably hit us before we touch ground."

CH 5
1968–*Omaha, Nebraska*

It was the era of Camelot, the beginning of a new age epitomized by President John Fitzgerald Kennedy and his beautiful wife Jacqueline. Back then I was the Camelot Kid. This was a time of great celebration among American Catholics. A few years earlier, our two Johns—pope and president—had captured the spirit of the age, each contributing in his own way to the cultural upheaval rocking society. In 1962 Pope John XXIII called the Second Vatican Council, which, by inviting active participation of the laity, radically changed the relationship between Catholics and their Church. Simultaneously, culminating in his death in 1963, John Kennedy, the nation's first Catholic president, called the youth of America to service by challenging, "Ask not what your country can do for you—ask what you can do for your country."

Like so many others, I was aflame in the passion of that time, imbued with the notion of freedom and social justice, acutely aware of my obligation as a privileged white American to those less fortunate than myself. As a member of the most entitled generation in U.S. history, I desperately wanted to find a way to give back to the country I loved. The president's assassination marked a turning point in my life and in the lives of so many others. Caught up in the passion of the time, I wanted nothing more than to become a white knight in service to my dead king.

Working out the form this service would take was proving to be no easy matter, however.

The problem was, my idealism was confused. The young president had been the Pied Piper of *both* the Peace Corps *and* the war in Southeast Asia, and as taken as I was with the cause of brotherhood and peace, I flat-out believed in the Vietnam War. My ideals may have been skewed, but I honestly believed that if my call to service couldn't be met through humanitarian outreach, perhaps it could be met by killing communists in Vietnam. It wasn't that I truly thought out the issue. Vietnam was simply the war of my generation, and I accepted it as inevitable. If asked, I'd have responded in the same way that everyone I knew would have, spinning off the domino theory and declaring that communism was the cause of poverty throughout the world. But this was a belief held more through the power of conviction than through rational analysis. I was well-versed in "official" explanations, and I swallowed the government's rationale on the war along with the Baltimore Catechism and the Boy Scout oath. Like most children raised in the '50s and early '60s, I had been trained to answer questions, not to ask them.

But one question I did ask—and continued to ponder deeply through my first three years of college—was, which path would I choose for my service? About the only thing I *was* clear about was that following my graduation from Omaha University I wanted out of the Midwest, and I was searching for a direction that would fulfill that goal. Prior to my senior year of college in 1967 I made the decision. The warrior won out. That summer I enlisted in a ten-week Marine Corps officer-training program at Quantico, Virginia. It was called the Platoon Leader Course, and if I passed it I'd receive a commission as a second lieutenant and be able to wear dress whites when I graduated from college the following May. If I failed, my name went back to the local draft board.

To prepare us to lead men, the drill instructors provided daily instruction in basic field maneuvers, parade drill, hand-to-hand combat, and the use of various forms of weaponry. They took us on forced marches, taught bayonet fighting with heavy pugil sticks, and marched us to classes on topics ranging from battle tactics to the Uniform Code of Military Justice. But their main tactic was administering ongoing physical abuse, including such inspirational teaching methods as bashing rifle butts against our helmets (heads enclosed), slamming us into walls, and balancing the tips of bayonets on our bare heads as we stood at rigid attention.

Our alleged mentor heading this academy of pain was Drill Instructor Dakin, a rawboned, perpetually furious Southern tangleweed who greeted us each morning at 4:30 reveille on the bank of the Potomac River. Screaming maniacally, Dakin was an avenging angel of death as he stormed through our ranks, jostling bodies like bowling pins, berating us for being maggoty infiltrators of his beloved corps. "Drop, scumbags!" he bellowed as our company of forty men stood at attention on the riverbank. In a single mass, down we'd go, slamming ourselves onto the dew-chilled concrete for push-ups. Then up, then down, up, down, up, racing into our barracks—*on the double*—to haul out our footlockers for him to inspect, then back to the barracks, lugging footlockers up the narrow stairs. Running back to formation, down for more push-ups, up, down, up, back to attention: "Ten-<u>hut</u>!!!"

Dakin was a master at picking out the weakest man and harassing the poor guy unmercifully until he broke down in tears and quit the program. In this manner, he hacked and slashed his way through our platoon for several weeks, eliminating one sorry excuse for a Marine after another in his frenzied mission to make us all quit and go home. Particularly effective among his many weapons was a morning ritual dreaded by all. It's not easy to remain invisible while standing at attention in a line of rigidly positioned men, but I fooled myself into believing I had been doing just that on the morning my name was called. Stopping before me, Dakin bent his lanky, angular frame nearly double so he could hiss straight into my face.

"Shithead," he growled, "git down that riverbed and grab me some pinchy bugs." The veins of his face pulsated like miniature volcanoes ready to explode as he showered me with spittle. "I'm gonna stick two'em up yer nose."

There was no choice. Into the weeds I went, desperately trying not to soil my starched fatigues in the fetid water, knowing too well the consequences of coming back with soiled "guv'mt propitty." As carefully as possible, I scooped up several of the primordial creatures that abounded there, slimy black pustules three inches long, writhing globs of swamp snot curling into tight, glutinous balls the moment I touched them. Running back to my screaming master, I juggled the putrid glop hand to hand, trying not to look. Standing ramrod straight, I presented my dank offerings and cringed at what I knew was coming. Laughing demonically, the raging sadist couldn't contain his glee as he squeezed them open in his long white fingers, dripping them like crushed lemons down my face. Wedging the thrashing wet millipedes under my helmet, inside my eyeglasses, across my lips. Begging me to flinch so he could "stomp your miserable little ass back to the shithole ya come from."

None of this made the slightest sense to me, but I was prepared to suffer far worse for my noble cause, so I submitted to the abuse. And truthfully, besides the physical abuse, the drill instructors had nothing on the Old Man back home, slinging plaster onto walls and bellowing for "more mud, goddammit, more mud!"

Dakin's brutality eventually alienated me, however. I could understand the concept of tearing us down in order to build "lean, tough fighting machines," but something died in me on the Monday morning he walked into the squad bay with an especially smug smile on his face. As we stood at attention next to our bunks, our drill sergeant proceeded to tell us how he had spent Sunday afternoon, riding his horse on the artillery range, lassoing the feral dogs stranded there and dragging them to death. I knew right then that I was done. It may have been that the diligent nuns had actually succeeded too well in my training, for I simply could not reconcile my call to service with such vicious behavior. But the one thing I wouldn't do was let Dakin win. Consequently, I hung on and after ten grueling weeks, I graduated at the bottom of my class—couldn't march in time and never passed an inspection—and was offered my commission.

But in my senior year of college, I turned down the commission. Years later in my work with the vets, I learned that the Marine Corps stands for honorable values that far transcend such insanity. But the spell had been broken. My idealism was still intact, however, so I opted to sign up with a Catholic offshoot of the Vista Volunteers (Volunteers in Service to America) called the Extension Volunteers. The training was scheduled to begin a few weeks after I graduated in June of 1968. On completion four weeks later, I'd be assigned to a small town in the Appalachian Mountains to assist at the local parish.

At that time draft deferments were allowed for teachers, and I could have stayed on in Omaha with a job at a local high school, but *that* was the one option I was not considering. Besides needing to work out my mode of service, I had known for years that if I were ever to find myself, I needed to escape the stultifying haze of the Midwest (so different in those years from how it is now). Embracing this newfound path, I was on my way.

Or so I thought.

In July I began the Extension training program at the University of Chicago along with dozens of other young Catholic volunteers from around the country. It was heady stuff for a parochial hayseed from Nebraska: daily Mass; liberal theology; and meetings with gang members, community organizers, drug addicts, politicians, and inner-city clinics performing miracles on a daily basis. The young men and women were as starry-eyed as I was, equally committed to creating social change, and I felt that I had finally found my tribe. The oldest was thirty, but most of the others were new college graduates like me. Three women to every guy and hugs all around. A bachelor's paradise.

The program was fascinating, but I found the real learning in my relationships with the other volunteers. I had never experienced such loving camaraderie, particularly with young women. In Omaha my buddies were jocks, good guys but hard-core in terms of what constituted acceptable masculine behavior. Anger was the one permitted emotion, tenderness forbidden, and a feigned toughness expected from anyone who wanted to be considered manly. With the Extension volunteers, the genders were mixed and mutual caring was the order of the day.

In a convivial coed group—pretty uncommon with my friends back home—we explored Chicago, riding the elevated railway through steamy ghettos, screeching past windows close enough to touch as we crisscrossed the invisible fault lines of race and economics fracturing the city. Oblivious to our blatant white privilege, we ran like bell-bottomed loons through the financial district at lunchtime, hung out on skid row, and went into the night indulging in the pleasures of Old Town's noisy coffeehouses and the lavishness of the Loop. Pure in our young hearts as we never would be again.

My great quandary seemed to have been resolved. I had found the perfect venue for my service and couldn't have been happier. It was so perfect, in fact, that there seemed to be a mistake when, in the middle of this communal bliss, my draft notice came screaming through the mail. But the only mistake had been the illusion that I was in control of my destiny. As it turned out, the Extension director had failed to register my paperwork with the Omaha draft board, which would have guaranteed a deferment as long as I was in the program.

So there it was. Whether through fate, administrative error, or simple bad luck, my first choice was not to be denied. The draft notice was crystal clear: on August 25, 1968, I was to show up at the Omaha draft board to be inducted into the United States Army. I had been so thoroughly infused with the values of my upbringing that it never occurred to me to resist. When Uncle Sam called, I went.

In truth, I was so driven by passion that it hardly mattered. The split was still there, and my values hadn't changed. I had chosen one path but was drafted into another. In either case, I still considered myself a white knight in service to his dead king and was more than willing to do whatever was asked. Getting drafted was just another ticket out of Omaha, so as with virtually everything, I trusted those in authority and marched ahead. Serve the poor, kill enemy soldiers, no problem. Like I said, I was the Camelot Kid.

And what a time it was! Society's cultural bedrock was crumbling beneath our feet, and the dust was "blowin' in the wind." A generation pampered like none other was coming of age as it wrestled with the mixed values of survival, duty, freedom, and sex. Being thick-fingered, tone deaf, and so shy I could barely look in a mirror, I might not have been able to play the guitar, but I was searching for my own role in the drama ripping through our country. The dice had rolled, and my vehicle to service was determined. Toward this end, the man who graduated last in his class at Quantico, Virginia, was finally, finally, on his way out of town. About the only thing I didn't have was a yellow submarine. But that's a different story. All I really wanted was a noble cause in which to believe.

As it happened, things did not work out that way.

CH 6
MARCH 13, 1969-*Vietnam*

All that night the survivors screamed.

It was my second day with the Company. That morning, a fleet of helicopters flew onto the field where we were waiting. The choppers descended in a roaring din, whipping up whirlwinds of dust as they hovered over the billowing elephant grass. Fighting through the rotor wind, we hauled our heavily armed bodies on board the doorless aircraft and were treated to a blowy twenty-minute ride to the NVA bunkers.

Landing in another field, we stumbled off the aircraft, dragging our bulky rucksacks, rifles, rocket grenades, portable LAW rockets, Claymore mines, shovels, picks, and 90-millimeter recoilless rifles (basically bazookas). I shared a collective sigh of relief with the grunts. We'd probably be in for a fight when we attacked the bunkers, but at least the LZ hadn't been hot.

We quickly moved into the jungle and started setting up camp beneath the stifling canopy. Then, as always, a recon patrol was sent out to get the lay of the land and locate the enemy's bunkers. What happened next would depend on what they found. Grunts were the ass-end of the chain of command, and they knew exactly how different their agenda was from that of the brass. The military command demanded contact and body counts; we wanted the NVA to not be home.

No such luck.

Within minutes the recon squad took fire as they approached the bunkers. Luckily no one got hit, and Captain Bates called for artillery rounds on the snipers. That was my first experience of "friendly fire," and I huddled behind trees with the other grunts as shrapnel from the 155mm shells tore up the jungle around us. There was no return fire, so another squad was sent out, but the enemy was nowhere to be found. It was likely that they were hiding out in tunnels below the complex. We'd find out in the morning, the CO said.

That night, after another glutinous C-rat dinner, three-man observation posts were set a few meters outside the perimeter. They would maintain our vigilance against a nighttime attack, which was considered likely. The grunts around my bunker sat in the dark, smoking and speculating on what to expect if the NVA chose to defend or come at us that night. The hope was that they had vacated the premises after our artillery barrage, but nobody was taking bets on that one. It was pretty simple, one nineteen-year-old corporal offered. "We're gonna move on the bunkers tomorrow," he said in a hoarse whisper. "They'll either be empty or full of pissed-off gooks waiting for us. If they're empty, we'll ransack the complex and destroy everything we can. If the fuckers are home, the jungle's gonna explode and people will die."

It soon became apparent that nothing was to be gained by worrying about the unknown, so we found our individual sleeping spots and settled in for the night. Awake in the darkness, I felt weird, lying so close to the enemy. I knew their mission was to kill us but couldn't help wondering who those guys were and what they were feeling as they stared into the same void.

The mortar fire started around midnight.

First there were pops in the near distance, then explosions outside the perimeter. Because of the heavy canopy, the NVA had no visibility and most of their rounds fell wide, rattling the surrounding jungle. A couple did land close in, though, and a piece of shrapnel hit one guy in the butt, giving me my first opportunity to treat a combat casualty. The explosions were followed by intervals of deep quiet. More artillery was called in, and we began back-and-forth exchanges interspersed with periods of eerie silence. This went on for a couple of hours, making it impossible to relax, let alone sleep.

Then KA-BOOM—the jungle erupted in an explosion that shook the earth. The mortar squad had moved too close to the observation post, and one of the grunts detonated the Claymores, unleashing a barrage of shrapnel that obviously found its mark.

The screams began immediately, first wild and panicked by the shock of having been stricken in the flash of an instant. Then mournful, afraid, as if calling out to a lost god or a distant mother. Our *chieu hoi* scout Kahn answered their cries, warning them to crawl in and surrender or face more fire. This quieted them momentarily, but we soon took fire from their AK-47s, and Captain Bates had two rounds fired from the recoilless rifle to suppress their aggression and prevent the wounded from escaping. The cannon roared, followed by a deep, penetrating silence that descended over the company, as if we were all holding our collective breath. But soon pain overtook the enemy survivors, spilling into nerve-splitting screams piercing the night.

We were told to stand down and get some sleep. But thrashing beneath my poncho liner, I couldn't sleep—couldn't think—could only stare into the black hole engulfing us all. The air was so charged, I could feel the intensity of the guys lying around me, their rustling sighs and snorty grunts. My entire body was reverberating in the roar of the cannon's blast, jolts of adrenalin twitching my legs as I tried to stretch out. Again it felt very strange to lie so close to the enemy, and I felt an unlikely kinship with the people we were about to battle. I still couldn't help wondering who they were and what they were feeling.

We went to them at first light, winding single file into the flickering shadows. As the medic, I was sent to stabilize the wounded so they could be shipped back to the rear for interrogation. Following the grunts, we wove our way through the thick jungle, and my mind reeled in its first exposure to my "noble cause," which had suddenly become all too real.

Twenty meters out we found the first, the one closest to the blasts. He was splayed out in a pool of coagulated blood, thrown onto his back against an upraised tree berm, staring vacantly into the morning sky. His green jungle fatigues had virtually disintegrated. Both arms were blown off at the shoulder, also his head. There was no neck. His dismemberment was perfectly symmetrical, arms extending a foot beyond the shrapnel-riddled body, connected only by threads of gristly flesh. The head was in perfect alignment with the ruptured torso, several inches above the amputated limbs. His eyes were open, blind to the rising sun, lips slightly parted as if he wished to speak. The skin was an unnatural gray. A mass of crimson guts spilled from the lower belly, and a single splintered rib poked through the gore of his ruptured chest.

Passing by the mutilated corpse, I stepped around the tree berm, following the trail, one step, two, three, then more bodies. Remnants of bodies: four shattered, liquidized shells splattered by shrapnel into great mounds of human pulp. Depending on their position when hit, the corpses were torn and broken at the extremities, the head and chest, the belly. Some may have been stooping when hit, some standing, their bodies exposed at various angles to the avalanche of shrapnel unleashed upon them. I froze, eyes transfixed by the flies swarming around each globular mass. Most striking of all was one soldier whose face had been scalped perfectly clean, ripped from a head that looked more like a shattered watermelon than something human.

Just beyond them were the wounded: five NVA soldiers whose bodies were too mangled to crawl back to their bunkers. And here, at long last, I found my call to service. With trembling, awestruck fingers I tended to them, oddly grateful to have something to do that might redeem the carnage. They were completely surrendered, limp and unresisting. It was difficult to guess their age, but they seemed impossibly young, hardly in their teens. Moving among them, I could hear the squishing of my feet sinking into the blood-soaked ground, and I nearly gagged on the sickly-sweet smell of bodily fluids permeating the air. I worked slowly, speaking in a soft, caressing voice as I gently set splints and wrapped field dressings, peeling away bits of shredded fatigues as gently as possible. Even then, I knew this tenderness was born of my own need for comfort, a desperate attempt to bring some small measure of sanity to an otherwise monstrous situation. I could tell the young men sensed my bewildered empathy as their bodies softened to my touch. We locked eyes as I worked on each man in succession, my breath taking a quick gulping turn as I encountered each new configuration of wounds.

Suddenly my reverie was broken by a loud whoop. Turning, I saw a grunt holding a ball of hairy tissue on the end of a stick. A dead soldier's face! Using another twig, he spread the flesh outward to expose holes for a nose and eyes below a ragged black-haired scalp.

"Whoa!" another guy cried, bending to examine the grisly find. "Motherfucker was ugly even *before* he ate the shrapnel."

Many in our company were celebrating our kills, laughing and joking about the "wasted gooks," but I was too dazed to participate. Looking at my new comrades, loose and joking now that the enemy had been ousted, I couldn't help wondering how many of us would meet the same fate as those dead and mutilated NVA soldiers in the coming year. This wasn't idle speculation. When I'd joined the company two days earlier, our roster stood at approximately one hundred and twenty men. By the time I was wounded ten weeks later, nearly forty percent of our number had been killed or wounded.

I got the prisoners stabilized as best I could, and we moved them to the edge of the LZ to wait for the medevac choppers. Moving away from the company, I squatted behind a large tree and lay my head against its gnarly surface. The explosions still rang in my ears, along with the haunting night cries. It didn't matter whether my eyes were open or closed, the images of those tortured bodies scorched my mind like blistered flesh. I had been with the company for less than forty-eight hours and already understood that I had crossed a line from which I could never go back. Not one of those sights, sounds, or smells, I realized, could be forgotten or denied. For good or ill, every bit of it would be with me forever.

CH 7
FEBRUARY 28, 1996–*Nevada City, California*

Suddenly the air exploded as my dog Lilly bounded onto the patio. Brushing against my legs, she dropped her rubber ball into the pool, scattering goldfish like bowling pins. I couldn't help chuckling as she sank her tawny Labrador paws chest deep in the water, her shepherd snout lapping noisily as the Akita tail waved like a flag on a windy day. Her sudden arrival shattered my image swirling in the water and my concentration along with it. I was glad for the interruption.

As always, Lilly was blissfully unaware of her effect on the fish. They were no less terrified despite this, and immediately reformed into a tenuous phalanx behind one of the bottom rocks I'd thrown in that year. Noting that the goldfish faced no immediate threat, I hoped their unfounded fear was an omen regarding my own journey. But there was one obvious difference: the goldfish had their little bunkers to protect them, while I was leaving mine behind.

Finishing her drink, Lilly walked over and tried to bury her sloppy jowls in my lap. Since I wasn't about to start my journey with soaked pants, I headed her off, cupping her long, fluffy ears in both hands and staring into those soft hazel eyes. Her gaze met mine with a look of unassuming innocence that I longed to share. But too much had happened in and after the war to fool myself on that score. Lilly stretched out on her belly beside the pool and quickly fell asleep. Her black snout hung over the watery edge, while her eyelids fluttered and snorts of spent adrenalin sputtered through her quivering lips. Her dewy eyes opened when I looked at her, and she whimpered as they focused on the ball floating on the pool's surface just outside her reach. I empathized with Lilly's frustration. Her dilemma may have been lighter than mine, but neither of us seemed likely to get what we wanted anytime soon.

Truthfully, I wasn't sure what I wanted, but I knew something had to change. There was just so much to ponder as I sat beside that pool. This was probably the most critical juncture of my life, and I felt powerless to find a way through. It had been twenty-seven years since I'd been in Vietnam, and now I was not only swamped in a family crisis, but my 50th birthday had just slapped me on the back, I'd recently been diagnosed with macular degeneration, my stress issues had severely exacerbated the arthritic pain from the old gunshot wounds, and I was being besieged by my subcontractors' staging of a palace revolt over financial issues. On top of all that, the VA was threatening to cut services because our success rate was costing them more than they'd budgeted, as more and more vets were flooding the program.

The main issue, though, was the pain and fragmentation in our family. Everything I had worked to build seemed to be falling apart, and I had no idea what to do about it. Going back to Nam may sound counterintuitive, but since the way forward felt blocked, going backward seemed to make sense.

I had often thought about my decision to go in the first place, and my route to Vietnam had definitely been a circuitous one. My compliance may have been due to the vow I'd made to my father in The Assembly, or just to the idealism of a young man struggling with the ambiguous values of the '60s. Or maybe I was simply too entrenched in my blue-collar macho mindset to see an alternative. Whatever the reason then, I now had a much different cause to fulfill, and even if I didn't quite know what that was, now was the time to find out.

CH 8
MARCH 13, 1969-*Vietnam*

The medevac choppers arrived, and the prisoners sailed into the unknown. Some of them would likely *chieu hoi*. I had no idea what would happen to the rest. Later that day more artillery was called in, and we located the bunker complex. "Locked and loaded," we crept in single file and well-spaced, expecting to meet resistance. But the bunkers were empty, as devoid of life as the bodies lying behind us. The bunkers' low doorways plunged into underground tunnels that we weren't about to explore, so we tossed in tear gas grenades, yelling "Fire in the Hole!" to warn each other of the impending explosions. I hung back as the grunts did their work, marveling at how ingeniously the NVA had constructed their edifice. Sculpted into the overhanging forest, the entire structure was fashioned solely from what the jungle provided.

After securing the outer area, we ransacked the bunkers, crawling through narrow sandbagged passages and small rooms, climbing tight little stairways into more rooms. We tore up the place as best we could, splitting sandbags, destroying the scant furniture and all usable objects. In doing so, we found a lot of stuff the NVA had left behind: tools, hammocks, clothing, knives, canteens, scattered ammunition boxes, etc. We even found a small brassiere, which was puzzling until Kahn told us it wasn't unusual for female nurses to accompany the troops in the field.

Several of the grunts pocketed small objects as souvenirs. My favorite was a slim green hammock that enabled me to sleep off the ground for a week. Sleeping was way more comfortable in the hammock, and I thought I'd found a way off the hard, prickly, knotted forest floor. But unfortunately, some guy in another company who had been sleeping in one got hit by shrapnel that would have missed him if he'd been on the ground. Word soon came down from the battalion commander: no more hammocks.

At one point Kahn motioned to the CO and pointed at a small hill on the outskirts of the area. Using a trenching tool, he dug into the hill and uncovered a five-hundred-pound bag of rice perfectly camouflaged beneath the sloping earth. The bag was exclaimed over, then doused with CS gas that rendered it inedible. I was told the nickname given to this toxic gas was "Charlie's sugar."

We hung around the area for another day, then were ordered fifteen kilometers west, where we came to a marshy river tributary. The water was up to our ankles, then our knees, and soon we came to thick, overarching bamboo blocking the way. We actually had to crawl on hands and knees through the bamboo to reach the water, then work our way across the stream, sloshing through the chest-high scum to the other side. From then on, it was the same routine for the next two weeks: hunt Charlie, exchange rifle fire, take a few sniper rounds, then get lifted out to engage another complex before being sent back to LZ Dolly.

The end of March turned into the first week of April. On Good Friday we were given a short in-country R&R at the Tay Ninh base. Lots of beer, a big outdoor swimming pool, pornographic films at night. And for some, the amazing Vietnamese reefer that came prewrapped in traditional cigarette packs (Winstons, Kools, Camels, etc.). These were indistinguishable from regular cigarette packs, each one sealed shut and holding twenty joints as round and perfectly formed as regular tobacco sticks. Then, on Easter Sunday, April 6th, it was back to the field. This went on with sporadic contact and short lulls, and we rolled toward the end of the month.

Then, on April 27th, we were flown next to another bunker complex, and our lives changed forever.

Our recon patrol was ambushed as it approached the bunkers. Within an hour we had lost five men who were killed outright, and twenty-seven others were wounded. As the company medic, I was called to the scene along with a platoon of reinforcements to engage the enemy and evacuate the dead and wounded. The NVA were pouring in rifle and rocket fire as we tried to get our casualties out of the large clearing, and people kept getting hit. It was my job to tend to the wounded and direct the medical evacuation. This required some heavy lifting, so I got a couple of grunts to help. Making the decisions on which guys to move first called for medical expertise I wasn't even close to having, but even so, I had to tell my helpers whom to get out of the clearing and whom to leave. The casualties had all kinds of wounds, both core and peripheral, and all we could do was get the least wounded out first, then tend to the more seriously injured. I slapped on all the field dressings I had, covering broken limbs, ruptured torsos, and head wounds; when I'd used all my bandages, I yelled at the grunts to give me the ones they were carrying.

The noise from both incoming and our own fire was deafening, the wounded were crying out, people were screaming, and when the CO called in our artillery, the explosive pandemonium ramped to a point where we couldn't even hear our own screams. Because we were so close to the NVA bunkers, the artillery rounds were coming in just meters from our position. A couple of guys probably got hit by our own "friendly fire," but the scene was so chaotic, it was impossible to tell.

At one point, as I turned to reach another wounded grunt, I stepped on the chest of a guy whose guts were spilling out of his abdomen. Tripping, I fell flat on my face. At that moment a rocket-propelled grenade whistled ten feet over my head toward the tree line where the CO and a lieutenant were directing our fire. My eyes were staring straight at them when the rocket exploded the lieutenant's chest, which erupted in a red geyser that momentarily obliterated my vision. I rose, crouching low, and along with the rest of my comrades, kept doing what needed to be done.

Eventually the artillery quieted the NVA fire, and we were able to bring all of our people out of the clearing and back to the company perimeter. The call went out for medevac choppers, and the grunts secured an area away from the enemy bunkers, which were still getting pounded by our artillery. The dead and wounded were positioned near the new LZ, and I continued to apply mouth-to-mouth resuscitation on three of the most seriously wounded. The choppers flew in quickly, meeting no resistance. We loaded our casualties on board, and they were gone.

The next morning, more artillery was called in, and with great apprehension we approached the bunker complex. They were empty, the NVA having disappeared into the vast jungle from which they came.

CH 9
FEBRUARY 23, 1996–*Nevada City, California*

There was one more thing I needed to do before heading out. The guys in my veterans' PTSD group had gotten stirred up by my decision to revisit the land of their worst nightmares, and I wanted to help them process their feelings. The group had been meeting for six years, lots of people coming and going during that time, and by 1996 we had a fairly steady attendance of around fifteen men.

They all exhibited various PTSD symptoms that created turmoil in their personal and family lives: depression, startle reactions, social isolation, intrusive combat ideation, sleep disturbance, flashbacks, rage reactions, etc. A few were white collar, most blue, and some had given up on the workplace altogether, living isolated lives on the fringe of society. Their average age while in Vietnam had been nineteen.

Tall, gangly Frankie had had to stand watch over a pile of uncovered bodies on a torrid concrete tarmac for an entire afternoon. He never forgot the smell, which was why he threw up when confronting a meat counter or the odor of grilling flesh.

Larry had been a tank driver in the Battle of Hue, and had literally run over groups of children the Viet Cong were hiding behind as they fired on the Americans. He carried the chaos of that street fighting home and lived an isolated life because he tended to erupt into rage at the slightest provocation.

Roy, who had worked in Graves Registration, had gotten soaked in blood more times than he could count hauling dead Marines off trucks. Not uncommonly, he and his fellow Marines would often pull bodies out of their containers to sit with them as they pulled a night shift. He could never forgive himself for desecrating these men, and he lived with self-disgust so strong that he relied on daily doses of alcohol and drugs to resist the urge to kill himself.

Gerald had used a knife to murder two women in front of their children while trying to get information on the enemy's position. Consequently, anxiety, fear, and shame overwhelmed him when seeing women or kids, so he became a "trip-wire" vet secluded in the deep woods to avoid all contact with the world. Gerald developed a habit of self-cutting and had drifted away from therapy after a few months because relating to Vietnam on any level threw him into emotional chaos.

Philip had been a triage medic ordered to do surgeries on civilians and enemy prisoners because the real docs were too busy working on U.S. troops. Despite his best efforts, his lack of training caused him to further injure several of his patients, and as a result he was never able to tolerate the slightest responsibility for others.

Sean was a chopper pilot who got shot down five times. He'd only received a few minor wounds but had lost a lot of crewmen, giving him a huge dose of survival guilt on top of his own traumas. At the time when he entered therapy, he had developed a habit of extreme risk-taking in his job as a state firefighter. Several times he had nearly killed himself while driving as he swerved off the road to see how close he could come to telephone poles. His deepest belief was that he had no right to be free from danger when so many of his young crewmen had died under his command.

We also had one woman, an Army nurse whose entire tour had been spent caring for the "crispy critters" on the burn ward. Connie, who had been suicidally depressed for many years, bore scars on both arms as evidence of her self-destructive impulses. Thankfully, she was also desperate to recover, and she worked long and hard to fashion a life that, though never normal, allowed her the emotional freedom to work within the boundaries of her limitations.

The group met in the basement of the county veterans' building, a long, narrow dining hall topped by an eight-foot ceiling, giving it a claustrophobic, bunker-like feeling that tended to stimulate the vets' anxiety, mine included. Our little band, dressed mainly in baseball caps, jeans, and t-shirts, formed a tiny circle in one corner, near the only door leading outside (an exit strategy insisted on by the vets, who couldn't abide the feeling of being trapped).

I wasn't sure what to expect that night. After each man checked in, I reminded everyone that I'd be in Southeast Asia for three weeks and that another therapist would be subbing. Then, as always, I asked if anyone had unfinished business from the last meeting. Big Harold immediately started in, rekindling an unresolved issue that clearly had the interest of the ten men suddenly leaning in around the circle.

"I still don't get it," he drawled, shifting his mammoth torso so slowly it seemed to move in waves, the hairy eye of his navel peering out beneath a ragged black T-shirt. Pausing, Harold regarded me dubiously while his ham-hock fingers thoughtfully stroked the wispy blond hairs decorating the folds of his blubbery chin. The big man seemed to be considering his words carefully. "We supposed to be the crazy ones, Doc," he finally said, motioning to the haggard middle-aged faces around the circle. "And here, you the fruitcake nutty enough to be going back to Vietnam." The last word lingered in the air like spent smoke, releasing vapor trails of memory linking all the vets present. Harold leaned forward, staring at me through puffy, squinty eyes. "Why is that, I wonder?"

He hadn't been south of the Mason-Dixon line in twenty years, yet Harold still spoke in a fluid, lilting cadence as soft as a Georgia peach. But the tone was challenging. It was a difficult question to answer, because I wasn't sure myself. I tried telling him I had never really met the Vietnamese. My combat tour had been spent fighting the North Vietnamese Army in the vast Tay Ninh jungle, far from any settlements. For that reason, something always seemed missing from my war experience. Vietnam had turned my life inside out, I said, and after so many years of processing my own traumas and those of so many others, I needed to meet the people of that country in order to feel complete. The skeptical look in his eyes told me he wasn't buying it. Harold had logged two tours slogging through the hamlets of the Mekong Delta. In this capacity he definitely had met the Vietnamese. Carrying scars on both his body and mind, he considered himself no richer for that privilege.

Hemming and hawing, I tried another approach, telling the men I wanted to test all my years of therapy and verify the emotional healing I needed to believe was real and not just a smoke-screen masking hidden fault lines that had disrupted my life in the past. This sounded good, I thought, perhaps even inspirational. But the incredulous stares of the entire group made it clear that nobody was buying that one.

"Hell, go to L.A.," called out Roger, a commercial logger who always dressed in razor-crisp khakis and was the only Republican in the group. "It's just as weird and you save the expense."

I then did something that's not always the wisest move for a shrink. I told the truth.

"What can I say, guys?" I asked them. "My shit's weaker than a dead puppy, and I really don't know what to do about it. Call it a midlife crisis, but the fact is, I'm losing the battle with my chronic pain and the VA just gave me a thirty-percent disability rating for vision loss. I'm scared, guys, and to be honest I'm fucking pissed. And if you want me to be really honest, I'm blowing it at home and have created a goddamn crisis in my marriage." The faces looking back at me were stunned, and I felt a stab of guilt for having obliterated even the appearance of a professional boundary.

"Hey, not to worry," I hastily added. "All I'm telling you is that I need a change of scenery to get away and work things out in my head."

The group remained perfectly quiet after I spoke. Such silence was a rare, usually uncomfortable experience for this group of traumatized men, and I thought that maybe I had reached them at a deep level. But then I saw Big Harold jerking in disbelief, his meaty, whiskered lips slapping against each other as he tried to voice a realization so bizarre it was screaming through his eyes. "I...do... not...fuckin'...believe...this," he finally whispered through gritted teeth. "People!" he cried out, flinging a fleshy arm toward his fellow vets. "Don't ya see? Doc's goin' to Nam for R&R!"

After the group ended, Harold walked over as I was putting away my session notes. Everyone else had gone outside for a smoke and some light conversation before heading home, so we were alone in the cavernous hall. The big man still seemed troubled. "Here, Doc," he said, reaching into the side pocket of his bib overalls. I tensed, knowing Harold was a man capable of having strange things in his pocket. But then he handed me a silver dollar. "You'll need this where you're going," he drawled, "'cause it'll remind ya of where you're from."

The coin was dated 1921. It lay heavy in my hand, solid with the values of a past Harold and I could only imagine. The face of Lady Liberty was stamped on the front, the phrase *e pluribus unum* forming a graceful arch around her steadfast patrician countenance. On the back was the figure of the American eagle, wings outstretched, In God We Trust set optimistically above the raptor's pointed beak. Harold winked at me.

"Keep it with you, man," he solemnly advised as he rotated his massive body toward the door. "You never know when it might come in handy."

Watching him leave, I realized that if any other person had just happened to have a 1921 silver dollar, it would have been surprising. Big Harold, however, was the man who used a Viet Cong flag for a handkerchief and a live hand grenade for a paperweight. I was glad it was the silver dollar he brought in that night.

CH 10
FEBRUARY 28, 1996-*Nevada City, California*

The sun was starting to sink, and I still hadn't moved from my poolside bench. It had been twenty-seven years since I'd been to Vietnam, and I still couldn't quite wrap myself around the notion that I was going back to relieve stress and work out personal issues. But there it was. Barbara and I had built so much in our twenty years together. Now the bottom was falling out in waves of pain and confusion, and I wondered if my initial skepticism had been right. Maybe I was going back simply to escape the pressures of my life. Maybe this search for healing was just a pipe dream. Truthfully, I wasn't sure, but I did know I needed to find out.

Brooding time was over. If combat had taught me anything, it was that when you move, move quickly—without hesitation. Rising with a snort, I spat into the water, slapped the blue Save Tibet cap back on my head, and let out a long, audible sigh as I prepared to leave the sanctuary I wouldn't see again for three weeks.

Barbara and I had just returned from doing a bit of last-minute shopping to complete my preparations. We had brewed a pot of tea, sitting in the kitchen to share a rare moment of tenderness before my departure for San Francisco International Airport. I remember holding her face in my mind as she sat across from me, studying her, breathing in the scent of her lotion, admiring the ripple of her laugh. We talked as we hadn't talked in a long time, holding nothing back as we discussed the issues that had overwhelmed our love. We talked until there was nothing more to say. Then I went for a last walk on the land while she cleared the dishes.

Turning now away from the pool, I found her coming out the front door, a slender, brown-haired woman comfortable in her own slow stride, meeting me with friendly, probing eyes long before our paths converged at my blue pickup truck. Her eyes showed concern but also seemed vaguely amused.

"I can't believe you're really going to wear this to a communist country," she murmured, straightening the bill of my cap.

"Fuck them," I said. "It's my hat."

Her body flinched, reacting to the defensive attitude I'd mastered over the last several years. Not wanting to spoil the moment's sweetness, I said more softly, "You know, honey, I really doubt the Vietnamese government cares much about Tibet. Or hats."

Her lips pursed and she nodded in mock agreement.

"And besides," I continued, "Vietnam hates China."

She nodded again.

"And besides that," I went on, suddenly excited at the thought of beginning a new mission free from the conflicts of work and home, "it's a free world. So yeah, fuck them."

"Right," she gently scoffed, taking a half-step back. "A free world."

We stood there wordlessly then, for all had been said and anything more would only exacerbate the difference between us: her desire to have a normal life, mine to battle demons and pull vets out of internal combat. Our true goodbye had been said in the kitchen. Now we found ourselves strangely embarrassed in the silence of our first real parting in twenty years. It was so clear to both of us; the need for this journey coming from the break in our relationship. The problem was mine; we both knew this. It was my job to untangle the knot I'd made of my life, and although I didn't know how—and certainly not why—the untangling was leading me back to Vietnam.

"I love you," I finally said, touching my fingers to her cheek.

Barbara looked me dead in the eye. "Love isn't the issue," she said. "It never was."

Taking my face in both hands, she kissed me full on the lips and whispered into my ear. "Go over there and find yourself. Then bring him home to me."

And with that, I climbed into the truck and pulled away. Before turning out of our long driveway, I glanced into the rearview mirror. She was still there.

CH 11

FEBRUARY 28, 1996—*Nevada City to San Francisco, California*

My plane wasn't leaving until 11:30 p.m., so I had plenty of time. I'd left early because my nerves were spiking and I needed to get underway, even though driving into rush hour traffic was antithetical to the withdrawn lifestyle I'd cultivated for years. My life working full tilt with the vets may have been an exercise in intensity, but at heart I was a beleaguered introvert with a public comfort zone the size of a postage stamp. For this reason, my biggest concern was how I would react to the teeming Vietnamese crowds. The guidebooks all mentioned how Western tourists often found the congested traffic and lack of privacy difficult, and I knew this would be a challenge, starting with the airport and the thirteen-hour flight.

I had been looking forward to the drive down for the last bit of solitude it provided. Like the entire journey, however, the ride turned out to be far different from what I imagined.

As I drove out of town, I just couldn't believe it was happening. Other than Nam, I had never undertaken a journey of this magnitude. My entire body was humming like a steel guitar, but the heavy traffic forced me into a single-minded trance as I cruised Highway 49 south out of the foothills. My route was straightforward, and I'd imprinted it in my brain since, at this time in my life, I couldn't afford to get any more lost than I already was. Highway 49 would get me to Auburn, where I'd catch I-80 West for a straight shot across the Sacramento Basin past Davis, Vacaville, and Fairfield to connect with Highway 680 South over the Benicia-Martinez Bridge (saluting the WWII mothball fleet languishing in the Carquinez Strait below). Highway 680 bypassed San Francisco Bay in a long southerly loop, and I'd be taking Highway 580 at Dublin, linking up with Highway 92 for a short ride over the San Mateo

Bridge to the southern peninsula, home of Silicon Valley and the San Francisco International Airport.

Fairfield is near Travis Air Force Base where I and so many others had reported for shipment to Vietnam. Seeing Travis triggered old memories, and it was around there that emotion started overwhelming my powers of concentration, flooding my mind with images of past horror and new dread. But this wasn't the time to obsess on matters beyond my control. Vietnam had turned my life upside down, and now I was not only going back but for the first time in recent memory had no one to answer to or hide from.

So I just started letting it all out, jacking up the radio full volume, singing, laughing, crying, talking to myself, scribbling my thoughts in a notebook propped on the passenger seat, oblivious to the surrounding traffic one minute, engrossed in the freeway spectacle the next. I must have been swerving quite bit because a few of the cars honked as they sped by. Caught up in my inner drama, I barely noticed.

After what seemed like days, the excitement began to wane, and somewhere between Walnut Creek and San Ramon I lapsed into a peace so deep that the concerns of past and future faded into the growing darkness. Time stopped, and I surrendered to the steady purr of the truck's engine buoying me in its comforting hum. For the last hour, I was borne along the highway in a soft stream of light that finally deposited me at a parking garage in Millbrae, just south of the airport.

The moment I cut the engine, anxiety jumped me like a rabid bat.

It was that quick. Leaving my truck was the point of no return, and my entire body suddenly locked into a resistance so strong I couldn't move my fingers from the steering wheel. I had the strongest urge to turn around and chart a course back to the sanctuary my family had once known, to wrap Barbara and Claire in my arms and undo the pain that had been done. But home was no longer a refuge, so sucking in a breath, I stifled my feelings and shoved the door open.

The shuttle bus was idling as I approached. I hoisted my backpack and climbed on, edging down the narrow aisle past a young couple engaged in an intense whispery conversation. The driver lurched into traffic the moment I hit the seat, and within ten minutes we were at the airport. I climbed off the bus, grabbed my backpack, and approached the revolving glass door leading to Vietnam. Although it had been dark for hours, the entrance was so well lit that the building actually glowed at ground level. Twenty feet up, however, the entire structure disappeared into a wall of darkness merging with the night sky. Taking a deep breath, I plunged ahead.

The main floor was sparsely populated at that hour, and I quickly made my way to the international flight terminal. Stepping off the escalator, I entered a cavernous hall that was a glaring bazaar of ticket counters, fast-food kiosks, and duty-free export shops intersected by rows of outlandishly colored plastic chairs. I took one step and froze, stunned by the visual onslaught. The drive down had been an exercise in self-absorption, a final bit of seclusion before confronting the throngs of Asia. *This* was Disneyland.

An imposing wall clock high and to my left read 9:45. Despite the late hour, the enormous room was teeming with people of all ages and races, some sitting, some ambling about. My fellow travelers represented an ethnic smorgasbord of turbans and saris, dreadlocks, suit coats, hoodies, blue jeans, and yarmulkes, and the air churned in a cacophony of foreign languages. The airline counters lining the walls were as diverse as the people: Cathay Pacific, Finnair, Royal Jordanian. If the scene hadn't been so heterogeneous, I might have stood out in my Jungle Jim khakis and Save Tibet cap. As it was, I didn't merit a glance.

After searching through the global plethora, I finally came to a sign that read:

EVA
SF - Taipei: Open 10:40 p.m.
Departure: 11:30 p.m.

EVA was the Taiwanese airline flying me to Taipei, where I'd catch Air Vietnam into Ho Chi Minh City. This circuitous routing was necessary because U.S. travel restrictions at the time made it impossible to book a direct flight to Vietnam, creating the inconvenience of having to arrange entry through Taiwan, Korea, Japan, or some other country servicing Vietnam. The counter was situated near the end of the room, fronted by more rows of tutti-frutti chairs. Two computer stations beneath the EVA sign were untended.

Only a smattering of people had gathered at that point, all Asians: a family of four, two couples, and a middle-aged man in a three-piece suit. They were spread evenly among the garish chairs, standing guard over their luggage as they checked and rechecked tickets against the posted departure time. I was still reeling from the abrupt truck-to-bus-to-airport transition and needed to limit sensory input, so I chose a seat on the side wall to calm my nerves and monitor the ticket counter. By the time my butt hit that chair, I felt like I'd been shot out of a nuclear cannon.

Except for the one I sat in, the row of chairs was empty, sandwiched between a Starbucks on one end and a corner restroom on the other. There were still a couple of hours before liftoff, so I settled in, maneuvering my backpack behind my feet and stretching out my legs. I was so tense that my heart was pounding and my shoulders felt wrapped around my ears. The tightness was not something I wanted to carry onto the plane, so taking a deep breath, I scanned my body and started a progressive relaxation exercise to relieve stress. This involved bringing focused attention to the various muscle groups—all taut as piano wires—and moving sequentially through them to ease the tension. I worked slowly, breathing in and out, tightening and relaxing as I tried to ease the adrenalin coursing through my body with every exhalation. After a few minutes I could feel my vital signs dropping from the stratosphere. Relaxing a bit made me wonder about the unexpected peace that had come over me on the ride down. I wanted the feeling back, but was afraid it was just the eye of the storm, a momentary reprieve between the chaos of my daily life and the challenge ahead.

Little by little, the chairs before the EVA counter started to fill. My fellow travelers were almost exclusively Asian, few traveling alone, all weighed down with various packages and items of luggage. There were several children among those arriving, some bright-eyed and excited, but most drowsy in their mothers' arms or slumped in the plastic chairs. The faces around me were as varied in their demeanor as people anywhere: happy, sad, tired, energetic, quiet, or chatty.

This was not how I remembered the Vietnamese, however. My intention may have been to aid beleaguered peasants, but that dream dissolved in combat. With one memorable exception, the only people I saw were either dead or wounded NVA grunts or the huddled refugees forcibly relocated from their villages to the barren landscape beneath Tay Ninh City. We'd see them as we flew in and out of Tay Ninh Combat Base, masses of displaced humanity sprawled around the hillside, an open latrine ditch snaking through their midst. Exposed to the blazing sun, the desolate peasants milled about like zombies with no identity and nowhere to go. They lived in makeshift shanty huts fashioned out of a squalid assortment of packing crates, cardboard boxes, and broken sewer pipes cast off by the American military. We'd zoom twenty feet over them, hanging out of the doorless Hueys to take photos, catching images of the poor souls cringing behind their flimsy structures to avoid direct sunlight and the roaring shriek of our choppers.

Every so often a voice on the loudspeaker announced check-in for a particular flight, and passengers at other gates lined up to begin the boarding process. Finally two EVA employees arrived, young Taiwanese women in crisp mauve blazers topped by pastel blouses and razor-creased black slacks. I rose with the others to present my ticket and passport. Actually it would be fairer to say I *bolted* to the counter. My sidewall perch had allowed a clear view of the terminal, and I spotted the EVA officials as they headed toward their station. Grabbing my backpack, I timed my movement to arrive as soon as they took their seats behind the counter. The moment they started firing up their computers, I was there.

My haste wasn't because I was trying to assert the privilege of an ugly American. Certain features of the journey were simply becoming all too clear, and I was suddenly aware that I was about to spend thirteen hours in a flying tin can several miles above the Pacific Ocean. The entire trip was starting to feel totally out of control. If I hadn't moved quickly, I'm not sure I would have moved at all.

The sleepy-eyed ticket agent greeted me with the weary nonchalance of someone who wished she were at home. I tried not to appear agitated, but I couldn't stop my fingers from tapping out a staccato drumbeat on the countertop. The young woman slowly booted the computer to life, her fingers crawling like half-dead slugs across the keypad. She finally got me checked in and handed me a boarding pass. The moment it touched my palm, I found a seat next to the boarding tunnel. Ticket in hand, I was ready to roll.

The line before the counter started to lessen as people got checked in, but there was no move from EVA to begin boarding. I was about to ask the ticket agent what the problem was when she picked up her microphone and announced that the flight was being delayed one hour. This put our departure date forward one day, to the morning of February 29th.

Leap year morning. Why was I not surprised?

CH 12
FEBRUARY 29, 1996–*35,000 feet above the Pacific Ocean*

Forty-five minutes later I was sitting in a window seat while the plane idled on the tarmac. The young woman next to me had explained that she had just finished her graduate studies at Stanford and was now going home to Taiwan to get married. She had taken a position in medical research, planning to work two years and then have a baby. It sounded good. Hearing her exuberant confidence, I envied the well-plotted structure of her life. I also couldn't help thinking how naive I had been at her age, expecting life to comply with my dreams. Maybe things would work out for her. I hoped so.

I was seated about halfway back in the plane, and as the other passengers filed in, I watched them shuffle down the aisle to find seats and stow luggage. Seeing the parents getting their kids settled, I was reminded again of how little I'd seen of Vietnamese culture during the war. I had no idea what I'd find in my three weeks there, but at least I'd come away with some new memories. Mostly I hoped to find the land as the news articles had described: a thriving new Vietnam enjoying peace and opportunity after years of devastation. It didn't make a lot of sense, but maybe if I could witness Vietnam's healing, it would help me find my own.

We were an hour and a half past takeoff time. The captain had just apologized for the delay and thanked us for traveling with EVA when the engines began to roar and we started our breathless charge down the runway. The plane lifted off with a jolt, accelerating into the night sky. As we ascended, a jittery silence came over the cabin. Eventually we leveled out at about six miles up, and after the fasten seatbelt sign was turned off, the flight attendant took orders for drinks and dinner. A blanket and pillow had been placed on each seat, and we were given warm washcloths to clean our hands with before eating. Tray tables lowered, we settled in for the thirteen-hour flight to Taipei. A fish filet and some vegetables helped calm my nervous stomach, as did the glass of cabernet sauvignon I sipped while trying to wrap my head around the realization that I was finally on my way.

My seatmate finished eating and folded herself into her blanket, shutting her eyes. Following her example, I did the same. The wine helped, and suddenly I was so tired that thinking of the future was a chore I simply could not manage. So I bunched the thin pillow against the window and allowed my mind to merge with the hum of the plane's engine, which was a sweet backdrop to the excitement draining from my body. This trip, I realized, was now beyond my control. Strangely, I felt relieved by that thought and gratefully rode the plane's steady vibration through the darkness outside my window. There had been so much effort to this point, so much planning and preparation, that it was actually a pleasure to give it all up and surrender to the ride.

The cabin lights had been turned down, and except for a few murmurs and the occasional rustling of small children, there was little sound from my fellow passengers. Engulfed in flickering shadows, I curled deeper into my seat. The dim quietness was comforting, but it felt odd to be so cut off from my fellow passenger as we soared together across the Pacific Ocean. That sense of isolation triggered twenty-seven-year-old memories of my time with Delta Company.

My mind drifted, gradually floating backward in time rather than forward. My first flight to Southeast Asia had also been a nighttime crossing. The outcome of that journey had been a three-month submersion in a depopulated jungle, fighting an unseen enemy with comrades I hardly knew. The medic I'd met on my first day turned out to be a "short-timer" who soon rotated to the rear when he was within a month of his date of estimated return from overseas service (DEROS). This left me as the only medic, meaning I belonged to no specific platoon or squad and was constantly rotating among units as the need arose. After my first two months,

I knew the names of most of the grunts but couldn't call anyone a friend.

That remained the case until close to the time I got hit. Once again, however—as with getting drafted out of the Extension Volunteers—forces beyond my control had intervened, creating two unexpected opportunities for friendship in a world largely defined by chaos and loss. In early May three new medics arrived on the afternoon supply chopper. One was a conscientious objector who seemed bewildered that he had ended up in the war he opposed; another was soon rotated home because of a family emergency; and the third was a short, cocky guy with thick eyeglasses and a distinct Brooklyn accent. This was Michael MacParlane, who had partied himself out of his draft deferment at St. John's University in Queens, New York. Since I was now the senior medic, it was my job to orient the FNGs and assign each to one of our three platoons. MacParlane was a jabber-mouth and, unlike the others, asked a lot of questions about me and life in the field, so we hung out rapping at his bunker. I immediately recognized a kindred spirit in him: he, too, was a Catholic and was equally drawn to Camelot and the civil rights movement. Like me, he had been educated in the liberal arts and loved to prattle on about virtually anything, particularly philosophical and religious issues.

War creates an environment where camaraderie builds quickly among soldiers, and Michael and I bonded immediately. Luckily the Company was experiencing an unexpected lull in enemy contact, which provided a more relaxed atmosphere with lots of time to talk. And talk we did. One of the things I liked about Michael was that he asked a lot of questions and seemed to genuinely care about what others had to say. During our weeks together we had increasingly deep personal conversations comparing life stories, how we got drafted, and our experiences with women—his prolific, mine negligible. It turned out that he'd heard of the Extension Volunteers and was interested in my experience in Chicago. Since he was the cause of losing his own draft deferment, he emphasized that I had lost mine through an administrative screw-up by the director of the program.

"Bad karma, buddy," he said. "Guess you were meant to be here."

I didn't know what *karma* meant at the time, but considering the winding road that had landed me there, I couldn't disagree.

Michael showed particular interest when I mentioned the gender disparity among the volunteers. "Whew!" he said, shaking his head. "Three women to every guy, and they drafted you out of that?" Laughing, he punched me on the arm. "Man, you got double fucked on that one, buddy."

Being from the East Coast, Michael was far more sophisticated than I in terms of both worldly experience and intellectual understanding. He had also been exposed to far more progressive teachings at his Catholic university. Another memory I have of those conversations was his scoffing at the biblical notion that mankind had experienced a fall from grace in the Garden of Eden. In my world that was a given, but not for Michael.

"Complete bullshit," he said, waving the idea aside. "There never was a fall. That was just the patriarchy taking over the Church from the women." Grimacing in disgust, he shook his head. "Christ would have puked communion wafers if he'd heard that crap." The man definitely had a unique way of expressing himself.

Michael was also one of the kindest men I'd ever known, although he had his own style there as well. He proved this one day by his willingness to listen to an issue that was ravaging my heart. In the Extension Volunteers I'd begun a romantic relationship with a young Latina from Colorado. Charlene (Charlie) Hernandez was a flamboyant free spirit who always wore brightly colored scarves and multiple bracelets dangling from both wrists. She radiated warmth and kindness, laughter rolling out of her in infectious waves that lit up every training session we had. Charlie's Catholicism was even more liberal than the liberation theology espoused by the Extension program. To her, communion meant those gathered together in worship, rather than the symbolic bread and wine.

"The Church is the people in spirit as the true body of Christ," Charlie would say. I had never met anyone like her.

Because her mother was Anglo and her friends Hispanic, she had confused feelings around race and wasn't sure she wanted a relationship with a Caucasian. We corresponded two or three times a week after my military induction, and I was desperate to have a fiancée waiting for me while I was at war. But she was hesitant. Over a three-month campaign of heavy persuasion, gradually I wore down her resistance. Charlie visited me at Christmas when I was home on leave, and at my insistence we planned to marry as soon as I returned from Southeast Asia.

This phantom union lasted until my second month in Nam, when the inevitable Dear John letter arrived, telling me she couldn't go through with it. She was too anti-war to be engaged to a soldier, she said. Even more difficult was the fact that her Mexican friends convinced her she'd betray her race if she married a "paddy." Her letter drove me into an even deeper sense of isolation in the Company. I desperately needed someone to share my grief with, but there was no one I felt close enough with to do so. I thought about writing home about it but didn't out of concern for my mother, who was already plenty worried about her youngest son. When Michael arrived a couple of weeks afterward, and when I eventually told him about my loss, he dropped his characteristic yakking and went quiet as I poured out my heart. He simply listened, his eyes intent on mine, occasionally nodding and saying things like, "Yeah, tough stuff, man. Total bummer. So sorry, bud." After a while, though, he stiffened a bit and offered this sage perspective.

"What the hell, doc," he said, "you're in Nam and might get blown away before you make it home anyway."

This jarred me and I was about to tell him to go fuck himself, but he went on.

"And hey, if you make it out of this shithole, you'll have plenty of chicks to make time with, right?" His voice was nearly booming as he urged me forward. "Look to the future, my man, look to the future."

For some reason, this helped a bit and we went on to talk about other things. One subject was combat—what I'd experienced and what he could expect. I was still working off the unfinished baggage of my youth, fueled by shame, and actually found combat to be a playing field I could relate to because it didn't matter how big you were or how fast you could run. All it took was the willingness to throw yourself into the fire, and as the Camelot Kid, I was nothing if not willing. Driven by a wounded self-image, I charged into combat with a passion born of desperation, throwing myself into firefights in a reckless, misguided attempt to assuage the shame carried from childhood. I told Michael that my sense of a medic's duty was to be close enough to break the grunt's fall when he got hit. Beyond that, I considered my job to be reaching every wounded guy regardless of the risk. This was a small man's bravado, completely nuts, and contrary to the military policy of having grunts bring casualties to the docs in order to preserve medical personnel. But there I was.

The lull in combat was not to last, and it was inevitable that we'd soon cross paths with the NVA. Along with every grunt in the Company, I wasn't looking forward to that contact and was still disappointed that my only experience of the Vietnamese was with enemy soldiers, not with ordinary people. It seemed bizarre that I had travelled halfway around the world to save this country and hadn't even met the people I'd come to serve.

I didn't know it then, but that meeting was soon to come, and it turned out to be a game changer that altered the way I remembered Vietnam twenty-seven years later. It was to this memory that my mind turned as I burrowed deeper into my seat, suspended between time, place, and my invisible neighbors.

CH 13
JUNE 2, 1969–*Vietnam*

On that afternoon I'd been hanging out at the CO's command post (CP) after the Company had been flown to a new cluster of NVA bunkers. The CP was a small group composed of the Company Commander and his two radio operators, an artillery forward observer and his radioman, and a few other specialists who sometimes traveled with the Company. This group basically made up our Company headquarters, and they always camped at the center of our nightly perimeter so they could respond in any direction if we were attacked. Captain Bates was on R&R, so Lieutenant Ashe, the Company's executive officer, was filling in for him that day.

I had gone there so I could listen to his battalion radio and put in a request for medical supplies. Suddenly the air erupted in a firestorm of AK-47 rounds pouring through the perimeter. We immediately went facedown and started orienting toward the attack. Luckily no one got hit as the rounds kept smacking into the trees around us. The lieutenant's radio crackled, and we heard that a surveillance squad had been ambushed as they were checking out the area. Following our standard operating procedure, Lt. Ashe told me to go to the attack area and take my orders from the platoon commander, who was already heading there.

We were cutting our way through the jungle when a grunt came stumbling through the trees. His right arm had been broken by an AK round, and he was holding it with his left hand across his chest. He'd been at the rear of the squad as they crossed the clearing, he said, and was able to dive into the bush when the firing started. His wound seemed pretty straightforward, so I slapped on a field dressing, tied his arm into a makeshift sling, and told him to find one of the other medics to check him out. Moving on, we made it to the clearing.

Two grunts were lying in a small open area—one shot in the head, choking on his vomit and sputtering into the bloodied dust. The other had been hit several times through the torso and extremities. The lieutenant at the site was a newbie who had rotated into the company around the same time Michael had. This was his first firefight, and he seemed flustered, almost panicky, screaming at his men to "Return fire! Return fire!" after they were already doing so. The enemy's bullets were kicking up dirt at the edge of the tree line, making it clear that the NVA were in trees, firing from an elevated position. Our casualties were lying flat, and I suspected they weren't visible to the snipers from that angle. I thought I might be able to reach them without being seen, maybe drag at least one out. With my medic bag in one hand and an M-16 in the other, I decided to give it a try.

"I'm going out!" I yelled to the lieutenant. "Lay down more fire to cover me!"

He screamed back to hold my position until they got the grunts out. But I didn't see that happening any time soon and was afraid they'd bleed out if they didn't get immediate attention. I started belly-crawling into the clearing. I was surprised when two other grunts joined me. They had both received highly specialized ranger training and were meant to add leadership and expertise to our ranks. I hadn't spent any time with them but was definitely glad for the support. When we reached the two casualties, I tied on some field dressings and we all began firing, eliciting a full-on barrage from the NVA.

When the firing let up, I looked over and saw that the rangers were no longer there. I caught sight of them disappearing into the safety of the tree line and felt the strongest urge to follow them. A spasm of gut-stabbing fear nearly overwhelmed me with its impulse to crawl away, and I felt myself freeze. At that moment a familiar voice came echoing from an even deeper place: "You do not run from a fight when a friend is being attacked," the Old Man had said. Not *ever*. "You stay and fight with him, regardless of the odds."

That was his way—it was the Viking way—and if I were to represent my father in this war, it would have to be *my* way. I stayed.

The firing continued, short bursts from the trees where the NVA was hiding, and me blasting off a magazine whenever there was a pause. After a couple of exchanges, I had my face buried so deep in the soil that I was snorting dirt. Another volley came in. When I raised my head slightly to fire back, an AK round caught me flush on the chin, shattering my jaw and snapping my head to the left.

I have no idea how long I was unconscious, lying face down in a pool of blood. Eventually I woke up gagging on the syrupy fluid getting sucked into my lungs. My neck was so sprung that my head was almost touching my left shoulder, and I kept going in and out of consciousness as our artillery shells started rocking the jungle. It went on like this for some time, sporadic fire from both sides picking up in intensity, then dropping off before starting up again. At one point I sputtered awake when I heard my name called. Looking up, I saw that Michael was at the tree line just outside the clearing.

"Larsen!" he called out. "Larsen, I'm coming to get ya!"

I tried to yell back to tell him to stay put, but I couldn't form words because my tongue was flapping in space between the fragments of my mangled jaw. The lieutenant started screaming at him, too, but Michael wasn't listening any more than I had. So out he came, crawling over the matted ground. All I could do was watch. He made it to my side, and our eyes met for one long moment. He had that crazed, wide-eyed grimace we all had when under intense fire. He reached out with a field dressing in his right hand to cover my jaw when—*crack!*—a rifle round snapped over my right shoulder, shattering his eyeglasses and blowing out the back of his head.

On impact, Michael's eye fluid splashed into the cavity of my misshapen jaw. For the next hour I passed in and out of consciousness, staring into his bloodied eye socket, listening to my friend suffocate on his vomit. The rifle fire continued—sometimes intense, sometimes not. During one of the lulls, I took the field dressing out of Michael's cold fingers and wrapped it around his eyes, tying it off as best I could with one hand.

Suddenly a grunt came speed-crawling into the clearing. He stopped at Michael's legs, grabbed one boot, and started dragging his body toward the tree line. Our guys opened up big-time fire to give him cover. My eyes locked onto Michael's blood-streaked face as it retreated across the clearing, becoming smaller and smaller as he was pulled away. Just before they reached the jungle, the field dressing unraveled and fell into the dust, limp as a dead snake. Then he was gone.

Sometime later the lieutenant yelled that they were going to throw out smoke grenades to create a diversion and get us out. That scared the hell out of me because I figured the NVA wanted to keep us pinned down to lure more grunts into their line of fire. If we threw out smoke, I was afraid they'd just start spraying the area with gunfire to inflict whatever damage they could.

At that moment I realized the next step was up to me.

The grunt beside me with the head wound was dead. I told the other one, "We gotta do it." I grabbed him by his shirt front and started dragging him over my body to face the tree line. He had been shot through the shoulder, arms, and pelvis, and I must have pulled him over those shattered bones, because he screamed like a wounded animal as I moved him. But there was no stopping, so I shoved my right hand against his ass and started pushing. He was a tough kid and he pushed with me. I pushed, he pushed, and we'd move inches, then a foot. We kept pushing, but I had to stop a few times because I was exhausted and coughing up blood. Then we moved some more, ate more dirt, and after an eternity of cringing at every burst of enemy fire, we finally belly-crawled our way to the edge of the clearing. I had to lean onto my right side to shove him behind a tree, and as I did, two more AK-47 rounds got me—one in the left shoulder and the other through the chest, puncturing my left lung. A couple of grunts grabbed the guy I was pushing, and I was able to find cover behind a tree.

A few grunts about twenty feet away had put together a makeshift stretcher by wrapping a poncho liner around two freshly cut saplings, and they yelled at me to crawl over to them. I started to but passed out again. The next thing I remember was being lifted onto that stretcher. Later I learned that one of the grunts—Adam, from San Antonio—had run through the brush and dragged me deeper into the tree cover. A couple of guys grabbed each end and carried me to a nearby field where a medevac chopper eventually picked us up. The LZ was so hot, the medevac pilots couldn't land until the area had been cleared.

Besides Michael and the kid with the broken bones, two other grunts who had made it out of the clearing with minor wounds were also loaded on the chopper. The medic on board, busy tending to his patients, wrapped field dressings around my jaw and shoulder, saying the docs at the aid station would treat the sucking chest wound. The medevac bird landed near a triage station, where I was immediately put on an ambulance and taken on a bumpy ride that rattled the pieces of my jaw like gravel. Thanks to the blessing of physical shock, that was the only time I felt any significant pain. The triage unit, a large tent filled with wounded grunts from other areas, was in a state of utter pandemonium, with casualties screaming in pain and medics trying to create order out of the bloody chaos. I heard a chaplain giving someone the Last Rites, then he was over me, swabbing oil onto my head and speaking prayers meant to ease me into death. New bandages were put on my jaw and shoulder, and some kind of seal that eased my breathing was slapped onto both sides of my sucking chest wound. When the medics finished patching me up, they told me I was going on another medevac chopper to the Army hospital at Long Binh.

When I finally got to the operating table, I remember a nurse holding my hand. Her touch was more comforting than I can ever say. Anesthesia was administered and I immediately sank into a dark well of oblivion, for which I was immensely grateful.

CH 14
FEBRUARY 29, 1996–*Taipei*

I fell asleep with a smile on my face, remembering my sweet time with the Vietnamese families. Though cramped in an airplane seat, I managed to get through the night with a decent amount of rest. Stretching awake, I smiled at my female seatmate, who looked bleary-eyed, rumpled, and clearly disinclined to chat so early in the morning. So I eased past her and made my way to the latrine to relieve myself and wash up. I was ready to roll a few minutes later when the captain announced we were forty-five minutes from landing.

At 5:00 a.m. we staggered through customs, the starchily dressed officials checking our paperwork in minute detail before passing us on. My fellow passengers and I were then hustled down a long, winding walkway to a cavernous hall that was virtually empty. Several signs in Chinese added to my confusion, so I questioned an older gentleman whom I'd heard speaking English earlier. He informed me that one doorway at the end of the hall led to the airport exit, but the other would take me to connecting flights. While most of our group headed toward the exit, I hoisted my backpack and joined those going through the other door.

The hallway we entered was at least ten feet high and, like the large hall, was as sterile and unadorned as a surgical unit, with gleaming white walls and a metal ceiling topping a beige floor. Feeling like a rat in a maze, I meandered behind the others, passing several unintelligible signs that led to waiting rooms for outbound flights. Eventually I came to an information booth where a young man in a crisp blue sports jacket directed me to the departure lounge for Ho Chi Minh City. The room was located down a series of twisting walkways, but since my flight wasn't scheduled to leave for nearly four hours, I was in no hurry to get there. Having just spent thirteen hours sitting on the plane, I needed to move and spent the next two hours wandering the corridors, stopping only for a cup of tea and a piece of toast for breakfast.

Although I'd slept fairly well, I was tired and sore from the plane ride, more emotionally numb than excited to have finally reached Asia. Jet lag was starting to frazzle my nerves, and I was anxious to keep going until I found lodging in Ho Chi Minh City. Hopefully that would be easy. My friend and fellow vet Opey, who had returned to Vietnam the year before, had put me in touch with a driver who was supposed to meet me at the airport. Quang was a 37-year-old veteran of Vietnam's ongoing conflict with Cambodia and had spent months in the jungle fighting the Khmer Rouge. Driving his cyclo—a three-wheel bicycle taxi—he was to guide me through the teeming maze of Ho Chi Minh City.

"You're gonna need somebody to show you around, homeboy," Opey had said, eyeing me with genuine concern. "Saigon's totally crazy and crowded as a motherfucker."

Opey had been gifted his journey by a wealthy pot-growing cousin who wanted to help him appease some of the ghosts who had followed the 18-year-old Marine home. Nearly three decades later, having come through years of serious addiction and destructive behavior, Opey was ready. He'd definitely paid his dues, participating in two inpatient PTSD programs, undergoing several years of individual and group psychotherapy, and looking himself deep in the mirror to make the changes that needed to be made.

His cousin, who had traveled with him, wanted to see something exotic, so he'd scored a bag of weed after landing and spent ten days getting loaded, hiring women for sex at every stop. Opey didn't smoke and had been married to the same woman for twenty years, so he had been left to find his own brand of exotic. That mainly involved talking to people, visiting areas where he'd served, and distributing gifts of toys, balloons, crayons, and notecards to Vietnamese children. The trip had changed his relationship with

Vietnam, he said, replacing combat memories with those of laughing children.

I finally located the waiting area for Ho Chi Minh City, where I found a few dozen individuals, couples, and families scattered around a moderately sized room with a low ceiling and a single podium next to the outside doorway. Except for a square pane of glass in the door, the room was windowless. Walking through the rows of interconnected plastic chairs, I noted that the Vietnamese being spoken was clearly distinct from the Chinese I'd heard on the plane.

As in the San Francisco airport, I sat against a far wall so I could observe the others without being conspicuous. For some reason, I was surprised that those around me were dressed much the same as people anywhere in America: mostly plain slacks and collared shirts, a few sport coats, and a couple of teenagers sporting t-shirts with the names of bands I didn't recognize. The one exception was a middle-aged guy standing apart and wearing a green camouflage fatigue jacket and a military-style baseball cap. I noticed he was reading an English-language newspaper, which marked him as a possible source of conversation. Our eyes met as I watched him, and I sensed interest. Figuring this was my chance to connect, I hoisted my backpack and walked over. His eyes followed me as I headed toward him. To start the conversation off, I asked if he thought our plane would be leaving on time. The man folded his newspaper under his right arm and answered in excellent English that it probably would. He then abruptly asked if I had fought in Vietnam during the "American War." When I answered that I had, his eyes lit up in a flare of camaraderie, and he introduced himself as Major Tony, making a point to shake hands in the upraised, two-fisted grasp popular at the time.

The Major, a short, compact man about my age, told me he had been an officer in the South Vietnamese army. He'd spent five years in a jungle re-education camp following the communist takeover, and had subsequently made his way to America among the hundreds of thousands of boat people fleeing the government. He'd done well in his new country, he said, beaming with pride. He owned two liquor stores in downtown Seattle and had a wife and two children there. Surprisingly, Major Tony also stated he had a wife and two grown children in Vietnam and was making his annual pilgrimage to see them.

"Whoa!" I exclaimed. "Doesn't that make problems with the ladies?"

This seemed to perplex him. "No, no," he answered, indicating the wrapped presents at his feet. "Wives have no problem. American wife only second wife," he said, and she was also family. She had come to America as a teenager, and according to Major Tony, had no problem with the extramarital situation. Such unusual arrangements caused by the Vietnamese diaspora were not uncommon, I later learned.

It turned out that, hearing the Major and me speaking, a few others who also spoke English were quite willing to share their stories. Most of them were traveling back to their root country from America or from other countries. Some were returning for the first time, having left Vietnam years earlier as child refugees. But others, like Tony, had made several trips between their two countries. A few of the kids were going back to meet relatives they had only heard about from their immigrant parents, and one lovely young woman was bringing her Caucasian husband to meet her Vietnamese birth family. Tony had not introduced me, but it was clear the others had tagged me as a returning veteran, or even as active-duty military. Thinking about this later, I concluded that, along with my khaki jacket, they had likely misinterpreted the Save Tibet cap as being some sort of military headgear.

An airline official finally arrived, and we were lined up to begin the boarding process. A woman who was about my age sidled up to me and asked if I had a hotel reserved in Ho Chi Minh City. When

I replied that I hadn't, she said her family owned a hotel in District 1—we could take a cab there. It would be a very good rate, she promised. I felt something predatory in her manner and wondered how big a kickback she might be anticipating. When I told her I had other plans, she seemed disappointed and turned away.

Finding my row, I plopped down next to a young man at the window seat. An elderly gentleman across the aisle leaned over and whispered that I was wise to refuse the woman's offer. "She no have family," he said, and she would have been paid a commission if she had brought an American to the hotel.

Soon we were in the air and, exhausted as I was, a rush of excitement was sparking my nervous system. From Taipei, it was about a three-hour flight to Ho Chi Minh City. Suddenly I was very aware that the next place my feet touched earth would be Vietnam. To ease my nervousness, I started a conversation with my young seatmate. He looked about fifteen but told me he was thirty-two and had come to America with his parents fifteen years earlier. He'd had a girlfriend before he left Vietnam, and he was going back for the first time to meet the daughter she had been pregnant with then. His English was quite good, and as we talked I sensed how nervous he was as he approached this meeting, not knowing how he'd be received by the mother and her family. I asked whether he hoped to bring his child to America someday. He seemed startled by my question, as if such a thought had never occurred to him.

"The future is unknown," he said warily. "It will be left to fate." This deference to preordained forces among the Vietnamese was a trait I came to find nearly ubiquitous in the coming days.

Sensing the apprehension driving his bobbing knees and twitchy hands, my mind went to Claire and Barbara. Our family connection had been my passion and priority in Claire's early years, and I felt a stab of sorrow thinking of our current disconnection. For this reason, the young man's dilemma touched me deeply, and I wanted to support him in embracing this momentous event. I told him I had a daughter the same age, and I hoped he would have a wonderful visit. I went on about the joy Claire had given me (omitting the obvious) and how great her first years of life had been. Assuring him that a daughter was a sure path to a happy heart, I elaborated on the gladness it had given me to watch my baby evolve into a little girl.

"What fun we had!" I said, tapping his shoulder. "You'll love it. Best thing ever for a guy." The young father took in my words with hungry eyes, desperate to hear something positive before he got swept up in his new life. I kept nodding and smiling, desperate in my own way to convince him it was true.

We soon retreated into our private thoughts, and I noted how little idea I, too, had of what I'd find in Vietnam. There was no agenda, not even a concrete sense of why I'd come or what I specifically hoped to gain from the journey. It wasn't even clear where it would lead once I'd left Ho Chi Minh City. There had been several options to consider when I tried to form an itinerary: the Mekong Delta, several beach areas, the beautiful and inexpensive islands off the central coast. There were lots of choices, but none stood out from the others—likely because my true need was for an inner journey rather than an outer one. In the end, it seemed that my situation was similar to that of the young father. I had started a process that was now out of my hands. Fate would be the guide from here on, leading me into experiences I couldn't yet imagine.

One thing I *had* decided was to avoid the area where I'd served my first tour. The bulk of that time had been spent in the jungle, an environment I'd gladly keep away from. LZ Dolly was inaccessible because of its distant location, and there was no point in visiting Tay Ninh, since I had never even seen the city in 1969. It became clear early on that, although this journey stemmed from the war, my route would take me on an exploration of the present, not the past.

Along with hoping to regain a rational perspective, my main goal was simply to meet the Vietnamese people and experience the culture the war had estranged me from twenty-seven years earlier. Beyond that, I hoped to reach the city of Hue, the ancient capital of Vietnam that was still a center of business and culture. One of my vets had given me a box he'd brought home from the war and asked me to bury it in one of the gardens gracing the grounds of the Imperial City, a citadel within Hue that had been an early seat of Vietnamese power. Johnny had served in the area as a second lieutenant and had witnessed an atrocity he found hard to relate, even to his fellow vets. I sensed his souvenir had to do with that, and I was glad to take on a such a mission in the hope it would relieve this good man of whatever was gnawing at him.

There was one other reason I was determined to visit Hue. Just outside the city limit was a Buddhist monastery that was relevant to the veteran community because its abbot had reached out to American Vietnam vets still suffering from their war experiences. These veterans, Thich Nhat Hanh taught, were only the fingertips of America's invasion, and they deserved compassion, not condemnation, for their involvement in the war. The gentle monk had opposed the hostilities, demonstrating vigorously for peace and reconciliation. For his effort, he'd been banished from the country and now resided in France. His monastery in Hue was named Tu Hieu, translated as "piety through compassion." How did he deal with the issues of war and PTSD? I wondered.

The flight attendant announced that we'd be landing in Ho Chi Minh City within an hour, and as the minutes passed, I felt an increasing nervous excitement. Taking advantage of this last moment of respite, I lay back in the seat and tried to relax before landing, hyper-aware that once my feet touched Vietnamese soil, I'd be encountering a whole new world.

CH 15
JUNE 2, 1969-*Long Binh, Vietnam*

As I sank into unconsciousness, the nurse's warm hand was the last thing I remembered. What happened then was something I have replayed in my mind a thousand times, and it still fills me with wonder. After being anesthetized, I sank into a formless void. Emanating from that well of darkness, a pinpoint of light suddenly appeared, spreading upward and beyond the operating table.

I found myself facing my body from above as I seemed to be rising up in soft, undulating waves. The light seemed to coalesce into a golden cloud radiating from above. All I wanted was to leave that bloody slab of flesh on the table and soar into the spacious light engulfing me. What happened then wasn't visual, but it was as real as anything I've ever experienced. I had the distinct sense of a formless presence in the center of that light, regarding me with an all-encompassing attention more loving than anything I could understand or imagine. That presence communicated to me in a way that was telepathic, not audible, flooding me with the realization that I could leave my body right then and enter into the golden light.

With every fiber of my being I willed myself to do so. But the soundless voice added one condition. I was free to leave, but I would have to return to that body at some point and complete my life's journey because this lesson was not over. My entire being revolted at the thought of going through all I'd experienced again, and with that, the scene vanished. The next thing I knew, I was coming awake on the hospital ward.

CH 16
JUNE 3-24, 1969-*Long Binh, Vietnam*

After waking up on the ward, I was bedridden for several days and, because I was unable to swallow, fed intravenously until a feeding tube could be inserted through my nose. My meal trays consisted of four bowls of liquid containing the four food groups and a funnel. My job was to attach the funnel to the feeding tube, then pour the fluid into it so the tasteless nutrients could flow into my stomach. I had a chart and was supposed to record the amounts, but I was so concussed from the impact of the head wound that I couldn't add the milliliters, so the nurses had to do it for me. After a few days of this, I had a second surgery and was told that as soon as I could take food orally, I'd be transferred to Okinawa. The Army had a world-class oral surgeon there who would set a metal splint behind my lower teeth to enable the fragments of my jaw to fuse.

In spite of that good news, I wasn't doing well. Along with the concussion, my neck and torso were so twisted from the whiplash that I could hardly make it to the latrine. A few days after the second surgery, I was able to walk a bit but wasn't motivated to do anything but rest. The nursing staff began hounding me to get more active and participate in my own healing, pushing an aggressive physical therapy approach, urging me to exercise, walk to the bathroom, and clean the area around my bed. All I wanted to do was sleep. This developed into quite a tug of war with the nurses, they prodding me back toward the world while I battled passively to stay as comatose as possible. They would stuff me into my government-issued hospital slippers and prop me up in a chair, but the minute they left I'd be back in the sack, drifting into my psychic escape.

With my head and torso so twisted, I could tell from the way other patients were eyeing me that I was looking pretty creepy— but that was just on the outside. The real freak show was going on inside my head. Peering through the cobweb of wires and tubes surrounding my bed, I took in the bloody circus of the ward: a parade of mangled bodies swaddled in plaster casts, tubes, and traction wires. None of it seemed real. Then I'd start thinking about Michael and all that had happened, and down I'd go, spiraling back into welcome oblivion. It wasn't just my wounds or Michael getting killed. It was the whole goddam thing. I had followed the dreams of childhood and found they all led to the same nightmare. Camelot lay in smoldering ruins behind me. I'd come to Vietnam prepared to make sacrifices, but combat exploded the known limits. The loss of comrades was to be expected. I just never anticipated having their body fluid splattered across my face.

In the middle of all this, after the tubes had been removed and I was fairly ambulatory, some Vietnamese were brought onto the ward. Two mama-sans and a few kids. Peering out from under my bedcovers, I couldn't believe what I was seeing. All around the world, through hell and back, with no personal contact, and finally here they were—the Vietnamese! Wide awake for the first time since being shot, I observed the scene with fascination. A young military policeman escorted them onto the ward. He and the ranking RN had an intense, whispery conversation at the nurses' station across from me. She seemed upset, complaining that the Vietnamese were dirty and didn't speak any English, but finally she signed the form on the MP's clipboard and he left.

One of the women, several years older than her companion, was a compact, matronly lady who stood so quietly she seemed bolted to the floor. The other was a pretty girl-woman in her late teens with a baby in her arms. Both were dressed in traditional peasant garb: black pajama pants, faded dark cotton shirts, and Ho Chi Minh sandals on their feet. The older woman had her hair pinned tightly on top of her head and was holding a conical straw hat in both hands in front of her. The younger had a mane of jet-black hair hanging down her back. A tall girl and three younger kids clustered around the two women, all of them staring back at the glaring hospital staff like animals in a zoo. A tiny wagon train circled against the world. A few of the kids had bandages on different parts of their bodies, so I figured that was why they had been brought to the hospital: shrapnel wounds. It wasn't hard to see the nurse didn't want them there. Even though the ward wasn't full, she put each family in a single bed and, immediately pulling the mothers away from the kids, ordered them to clean the latrines.

Later in the day I drifted out of my usual stupor and noticed the young mother walking with her baby past my bed. There weren't any nurses around—not unusual at that time of day—just an enlisted orderly mopping the floor. He was a skinny guy, older than most of the patients, probably a lifer. As she passed by, he turned and thrust the blunt end of his mop deep into her crotch from behind. The girl jumped as if hit by an electric shock, nearly dropping the baby as she straddled the wooden shaft for one sharp moment. Struggling to keep from falling, she clutched the child into her right armpit and cringed away from the orderly, hooking her left arm in front of her face and chattering off a stream of angry Vietnamese.

"Aw, c'mon, *mama-san*," the orderly crooned, his voice dripping with lewd vulgarity as his right hand dipped to his crotch, pumping the loose folds of his hospital fatigues to imitate jerking off. "Boom-boom, baby. You and me, boom-boom."

Like a startled deer, she darted past him, scuttling back to the frail safety of her family at the end of the ward. It was over in a moment, but the spark of terror on that girl's face burned like a camera flash behind my startled eyes. Unable to deal with any of it, I plummeted back into my hypnotic slumber.

The next morning the Red Cross worker came around, pushing his cart loaded with books, stationery, and a huge bowl of brightly wrapped candy. He was a fat, middle-aged guy with a purplish alcoholic nose, dressed in well-pressed Jungle Jim khakis that did nothing to disguise the probability that he'd been out boozing all night.

Sometimes he'd talk a bit and try to be friendly, but mostly he was just tired and hungover, handing out his packaged goodies like an embittered spinster on Halloween. When they saw the candy, the kids' eyes nearly popped out of their heads. They clustered around the cart, tugging at the guy's trousers, but he just waved them away.

"No, this for GIs, not you. Beat it, now. *Di di mau. Di di mau.*"

That was the last straw.

Hauling my sorry ass out of bed, I shuffled over to the cart and motioned the kids back, cuffing them around as casually as I had done to my nephews and nieces back home, until they stood before me in a fidgety, wide-eyed row. Starting with the oldest girl, I used my hands to show them how to take hold of their t-shirts at the bottom and raise them like aprons to form large pockets. It took a minute, because the smallest boy kept trying to pull his shirt over his head, but as soon as they got it, I dug both hands into the bowl and loaded them down with as much candy as they could carry. When those kids saw all that sugar coming, their eyes flared like slot machine cherries and they went into giggling fits, squealing and hopping around. Behind us, the Red Cross guy sputtered angrily, as though I were emptying his personal bank account. We ignored him.

I then took a pen and stationery from the cart and walked the kids back to their beds. Standing next to the two women, I stared at the orderly who was lounging nearby, leaning on his broom and trying to make eye contact with the young mother. Sweeping my right palm in front of me, I made a hand gesture that said *enough*, and wrote out on the stationery: "Leave them alone or I'll report you." I walked over and tried to hand him the note, but he wouldn't take it. He just glanced at the writing, smirked, and slowly shook his head. I shoved the paper in front of his face, then dropped it, staring him in the eye as it fluttered to the floor. Finally he just raised his eyebrows as if I were nuts, turned, and walked away.

Overdosed by this brief foray into the world, I tottered back to bed.

That afternoon I was still burrowed under the covers when I heard the patter of many feet. Grudgingly, I opened my eyes and saw that all the Vietnamese had gathered around my bed. Before I knew it, several little hands were pulling down the covers and urging me up, their low murmuring voices calling me to them. Startled at this intrusion into my sanctuary of private grief, I lurched away. But this didn't seem to offend them, and they continued drawing me outward, dozens of feathery little fingers tugging, prodding, lifting, gathering me into my bathrobe, then forming themselves around me like new skin. Supporting both of my elbows, they folded me into their midst as we slowly made our way down the long corridor to the door. When we got outside, they pulled some chairs off to one side of the lounging porch, and we formed a tight little circle, pulling in against the war, the military, and all the sorry circumstances that had brought us there.

We sat on that porch for an hour, enjoying the shade from the midday heat, ensconced in our own world under the canopied veranda as the never-ending parade of wheelchairs, stumps, and hospital gurneys bustled around us. My new friends seemed barely to notice. Chattering away in their nasal singsong Vietnamese, they somehow included me through bright-eyed smiles and pats on the hand. The women and the older girl were friendly, though physically reserved, but the kids quickly bounced out of their initial shyness and started climbing up on my lap, sticking their faces into mine, touching my hands, my dog tags, my round eyes, screeching hilariously as they cocked their heads crookedly in imitation of my own. Over and over again, especially when I tried to communicate by sign language or pidgin Vietnamese, the whole group would break into fits of hysterical giggling, as if I were the funniest thing they'd ever seen. Mostly, they treated me like one of their own.

This ritual was repeated every day until I was shipped to Okinawa. In the morning I'd score candy and various knick-knacks for the kids, and in the afternoon they'd all come to collect me from my reclusive hideaway. Sometimes my inertia was overwhelming, and I'd push them away, clinging to the oblivion I still craved. But like the first time, they breezed right through my feeble resistance, clucking in soft insistence as their fingers peeled away the bed covers, gently feeling along layers of isolation, guiding me back into the world.

We never did work out a way to speak, hardly a single word. But our contact created a true sanctuary in a world of insanity and violence. Their acceptance transformed my depression, and because of them my last memories of Southeast Asia were ones of connection and caring rather than of despair. I'll always remember their kindness, and I live in the hope that our time together made some difference in their lives as well.

CH 17
JULY 1969-*Okinawa*

Three weeks after landing in the Long Binh hospital, I had regained the ability to swallow and was flown to the military hospital on Okinawa. The transfer order came abruptly, while my Vietnamese friends were off the ward undergoing medical procedures for the kids. I was bummed to the core not to have a chance to say goodbye, but I knew that was the military way: orders came and people moved.

My jaw was still wired shut, but that was a temporary measure until the renowned oral surgeon on Okinawa could fit me with a metal splint behind my lower teeth. This was a state-of-the-art surgery that would hold the fragments firmly in place as they re-fused. At the hospital I was checked in, assigned a bed on a ward, then taken to meet the magician who would perform the surgery. Colonel McCaffy was around fifty, tall and angular, an intense and cranky guy with the sensitivity of a bedbug. But his skill was unbelievable. The operation was a total success, but not without a dramatic moment that I'll never forget.

The extent of McCaffy's temper became apparent during the procedure as I reclined in the dentist chair, anesthetized but partially awake while he worked the metal splint into my mouth. My jaw, which had been unwired for the surgery, was frozen but tender to the touch. Midway through the procedure, he dropped a surgical tool on the floor.

"God dammit!" he roared, kicking the instrument as hard as he could against a wooden cabinet. He froze for one long moment, his body rigid as a stick. He then turned back to me, seemingly unperturbed as he resumed probing my fragile jaw. I don't think he noticed the wariness in my eyes as he continued wiring in the splint. For years afterward, whenever I'd go to a new VA dental clinic, the dentist would be blown away viewing the X-rays of my shattered jaw, and would call in the other dentists to *ooh* and *ahh* over the incredible result of the surgery. I will always be grateful for the superb treatment I received on Okinawa.

The hospital was a huge multi-storied building with a rooftop lounge area, which played a key role later in my stay. I was scheduled to be there a month before being rotated through Japan on the way home. It took a couple of weeks before the surgery was performed, and I was basically given the run of the hospital when not called in for medical appointments.

Roaming the halls one day, I saw the grunt whose arm I'd bandaged on June 2nd before reaching the clearing. I didn't remember his name since we hadn't related much, but we recognized each other as we were shuffling down the hallway and immediately struck up a conversation. His arm was in a cast, but he looked well and expressed huge relief that his wound was getting him sent home soon. He told me that the guy I'd crawled out of the clearing with was on the orthopedic ward and took me to see him. His name was Peters, and he was bedbound with a traction cable elevating one leg. Though we'd never met before June 2nd, we had a friendly reunion, reminiscing about the firefight, Michael, and the extent of our wounds. He thanked me profusely for staying with him that day. Along with finding him alive, that was the only reward I needed.

Occasionally patients received passes to go into the local town, and after a couple of weeks I decided to give it a whirl, so I caught a cab with another guy to see the sights. My energy was still flagging, but I craved time away from military overview. Also, since I'd had so little exposure to civilians in Vietnam, at least I wanted to taste what life was like on Okinawa. When we reached town, though, those sights turned out to be pretty disappointing: a string of bars, liquor stores, pawn shops, seedy cafés, and colorful little markets selling everything from live hens to bubble wrap. My buddy wanted to walk around, but I wasn't up for a hike, so I told him I'd get a beer at one of the bars and we could meet later.

Strolling up the block, I saw some young men loitering on a street corner, and I noticed that they were observing me intensely. That caught my attention because there was no question that their faces conveyed pure hatred. I nearly flinched at the unexpected animosity. Months later, doing research on the Vietnam War and American foreign policy, I realized that the U.S. military had occupied Okinawa since World War II, which incurred the wrath of the native population, who had already suffered from being invaded by the Japanese. Taken aback, I entered one of the bars to escape such negative scrutiny.

Like the other buildings on the block, this one suffered from peeling paint and overall neglect, making it look like a typical skid row bar in any large city. It was empty except for what appeared to be a middle-aged woman tending bar. When I ordered a beer, she served it with a knowing smile and a wink. I took a sip and was perusing the drab interior when I heard a rustle beside me and saw that the bartender had taken the seat next to me. At that moment I became very conscious that her hand was in my lap, stroking the area around my groin. She had undone the bun holding her hair, and I saw that she was younger than I had first thought, probably in her mid-30s. This was a new experience for a 23-year-old virgin, and I was anything but sure of what to do next. I needn't have worried, because my hostess had things well under control, and taking me to a back room was *not* on her agenda. We chatted for a while, her fingers moving around my crotch, but it wasn't a conversation, only my companion's inane comments about how handsome I was as she encouraged me to drink up and order more beer.

Her touch was exhilarating, but I'd been told by one of the hospital orderlies that the bar girls would fondle GIs all night as long as they kept paying, but most were not prostitutes. That was fine by me, since I didn't have the energy or inclination to initiate sex under those conditions.

I couldn't handle much alcohol, and after the second beer, I told my companion I couldn't drink any more, which, unsurprisingly, caused her to go back behind the bar. Before long, a couple of Army guys came in and sat at a table. I saw the bartender rubbing herself against one of the men as she took their orders, and I realized it was time to leave.

I found my buddy on the street, and he told me there was a carnival happening down one of the side blocks. We decided to check it out. Walking down the street, we could see an empty lot at the end with people milling beneath a few drooping banners. Reaching the lot, we found that the "carnival" consisted of only a few cheap rides, a couple of gambling stalls, and some food and beer stands. What we did find was a group of men, both Okinawan and American, gathered in the back corner.

We soon discovered that the only side show of this "carnival" was a fight to the death between a cobra and a mongoose. An Okinawan man was collecting admission fees from the ring of spectators, and he offered a wager to anyone who thought the snake would prevail. We didn't take the bet but did pay the fee, and gathered with about twenty others, all men, behind a roped off area. Eventually the snake was let loose in the center of the circle. It looked like some kind of cobra and was about four feet long. It immediately tried to crawl away, but the handler kept edging it back with a long stick. Then a mongoose was dropped a couple of feet away. Immediately, both animals tensed and prepared for battle, the serpent uncoiling its head to face the rodent, and mongoose circling intently around the reptile.

The viper feigned a couple of false strikes, holding the mongoose at bay, and it seemed like it might be a protracted contest. But in a flash, it was over. The mongoose had lured the snake a bit too far forward, then bit it behind the head in a lightning-quick attack.

We watched as the mongoose defanged the snake before the handler put it back in its cage. The "battle" had hardly taken a minute.

Before long we were back in a cab, since we had to reach the hospital before curfew. I had been titillated by the spectacle, but also grossed out by entertainment requiring the death of an animal for human enjoyment. Raised with my dad's passion for athletics, especially boxing, I found that I no longer had the stomach for blood sports, which only added to the estrangement between the Old Man and myself.

I'm profoundly grateful that we found a way to minimize our differences without a protracted battle that would have destroyed our relationship. It was never easy after Vietnam, and worsened considerably when I grew out my hair and joined the Vietnam Veterans Against the War, but we maintained a caring relationship until his death in 1976.

The highlight of my stay on Okinawa—other than the remarkable surgery—came on July 20, 1969, when the first Apollo space capsule landed on the moon. The outdoor lounge on top of the hospital was opened to any and all who dared to brave the mob as Neil Armstrong took his first lunar steps. I remember how odd it felt on the roof with doctors and nurses mixed in with patients and hospital staff, all witnessing the monumental event together. It was as if, for this one evening, the whole notion of rank was suspended as we stood in a close-knit group, staring at the incredible night orb that would never again appear the same. I thought how weird it was that our species had the smarts to get to the moon but couldn't find a way to coexist with our neighbors on Earth.

But the moon wasn't the only thing that was now different. I'd come into the hospital with a positive attitude, and for a few days that had worked. After meeting the surgeon, there was a two-week wait for the procedure, which meant I had a lot of time on my hands. That time was mostly spent thinking—my mind increasingly swamped with intrusive images of past firefights, particularly those from June 2nd. After getting hit, I'd been pretty much in shock and despair during my three-week hospitalization at Long Binh. Meeting the Vietnamese families had lifted my spirits, and I was hopeful that my recovery would be easier from then on. But it was on Okinawa that I started noticing that something had changed.

For one thing, I couldn't shake the sense of being under threat of attack. Jittery and watchful, I'd have startle reactions when I passed soldiers in camouflage fatigues. I could sleep only a few hours at a time, and I broke into a cold sweat whenever I was in the confines of an elevator. And I wasn't the only one. The other soldiers in the hospital joked about how easily spooked we were. Our nervous systems remained "locked and loaded" weeks after the firefights—for us—had ended. In our blue Army-issue PJs, we lay about the drab ward for days at a time, having little to do in the intervals between chow and treatment procedures but read, play cards, and tell stories. Pretty much everyone had tales of combat, most as gruesome as mine. Others, like the rear-echelon Master Sergeant who broke his jaw on a diving board at the NCO club, had stories that were less interesting. Our young bodies, where possible, healed quickly, leaving the mind to ponder its own scars.

My surgery had been completed a few days before the moon landing, and a week after the procedure I was scheduled to be medevacked to Japan for a night or two as I rotated back home. We'd be flown on an Air Force jet, and even though my jaw was now wired to a splint, the nurse made me get out to the plane on a stretcher. Most of the other patients were ambulatory and seated upright, and I felt irritated at not being allowed to walk out on my own power. That cloud had a silver lining, however, and I soon appreciated the fact that my horizontal status gave me more time with the lovely young nurse who was tucking me in with extra blankets and pillows.

It was a three-hour ride, and before long we were piling out of the plane onto the bus that would transport us to an Air Force hospital. Leaving the terminal, we encountered typical Asian traffic, a cacophonous, fume-spewing nightmare of cars, trucks, and motorcycles. Suddenly—*bang!*—a car next to us backfired and forty wounded grunts dove onto the floor. For several moments there was utter stillness. Eventually a twitter of laughter rose from the silence, followed by a clumsy reshuffling as we pulled ourselves from the floor, rising sheepishly, untangling from the scattered mess of crutches, spilled soda cans, and magazines. Previously we had been a group of strangers randomly routed in the medevac channel to the States. But now a flare of recognition sparked among us as we settled back into the false comfort of our seats, straining to clear the air with nervous laughter and feeble curses.

This seemed a signature event even then, giving us all a taste of what we were leaving behind. For some, however, it was a warning of things to come.

CH 18
JULY 1969-APRIL 1970-*Fort Riley, Kansas*

Ten months in the Fort Riley, Kansas, hospital allowed me ample opportunity to reflect on what I'd experienced in Vietnam. Along with wrestling with memories, I was able to observe the other wounded GIs. They were kids mostly, young draftees like me mixed in with a smattering of lifer types. I was one of the old ones at twenty-three. The others, those without pimples, represented an astonishing variety of stories about how they had been caught in the war.

Here, too, I knew from being startled awake that others also had nightmares. And the difference was still talked about as we passed time, counting the months to discharge. I was due for a couple more surgeries on my jaw, to be spread out over several months, and would then be given what the Army called the five-month early out. One of the military's only policies that made sense to most of us, it was designed to allow wounded soldiers to be released early once their medical treatment was completed. After all, there's no sense in keeping soldiers on active duty when they have only a few months left to serve.

As I think back on it, the military had a "don't ask, don't tell" policy even then, but it related to combat trauma. Although the physical care was excellent, care of the mind and emotions simply did not exist. People were returning from tours where they had undergone an ongoing barrage of horror, and no one even asked if they experienced psychological repercussions. The GIs, anxious to be discharged as soon as possible, did not tell.

There were several reasons for this disinterest in treatment. Nothing the Army provided, except chow, was to be trusted, and certainly no one I knew wanted some Army shrink mucking around inside his head. In truth, the guys I knew wanted the Army *out* of their heads. For many, the drugs of all kinds that were rampant throughout the hospital provided a temporary, misguided relief from symptoms. There was a beer canteen in the ambulatory barracks, and marijuana was everywhere. Speed and psychedelics were available to anyone so inclined. Topping off this arsenal were the opioids and other treats pilfered from the pharmacy by GIs turning drugs over for cash.

Our training was another factor that contributed to ignoring alarming emotional symptoms, since the military had taught us to control emotion at all costs. Downplaying psychological symptoms was not that different from sucking up a weekend hangover for Monday reveille. And we were young men raised in the way of our fathers: we were *expected* to suffer in silence.

This is not to say that every soldier turned into a druggie or developed PTSD. Most of the patients I knew appeared surprisingly normal, considering their wartime experiences. Chaplains were available, and many of my comrades seemed to find guidance and comfort in traditional religion. The lucky ones also had family support, which made readjustment easier during those years of personal and social unrest. As noted, however, exceptions abounded, and VA studies later revealed that many thousands of these young veterans carried away time bombs set to explode under future conditions.

Smokey Joe is the man who comes to mind when I think of those days. Smokey was a tall, redheaded, skin-and-bone Okie stoner who got hit by a chunk of shrapnel in his lower back, which left him gouged like a pitted peach and listing to one side. As a result, it was a huge challenge for him to manage the long walk from the ambulatory barracks up the hill to the hospital.

"If it hadn't been for marijuana," Smokey declared, "I never would have made it out of Nam, let alone this sorry shit."

Several of us walked with Smokey in the mornings. Hiking to our assigned jobs at the hospital—always in those damn blue pajamas—we would take turns pushing him from behind, supporting him in his struggle to avoid getting moved to a more restrictive inpatient ward.

It was Smokey who best put words to the dilemma some of us were experiencing. "Ohhhh, man," he crooned over and over one night, muttering mostly to himself as we sat around the barracks after a night of beer, reefer, and war stories. "Just can't let it go, ya know? Know what I mean?" His eyes suddenly lit up in a burst of panic. "Can't let it go!" he cried. "Can't let it go!"

As he spoke the rest of us nodded like addicts hooked on the same needle. We were buzzing more from the shock of memory than from the booze and weed, knowing all too well the feeling—if not the name—of the chaos and turmoil locked within our bodies (PTSD was not a recognized disorder until 1980).

CH 19
MARCH 1, 1996-*Ho Chi Minh City, Vietnam*

The plane landed at Tan Son Nhat Airport, and as it taxied down the runway, I noticed several small, three-walled concrete structures. I knew from my research that these were left over from the war—constructed to protect American choppers from shrapnel exploding from Viet Cong mortar rounds. As we came to a stop near the terminal building, we were instructed to exit the plane and line up at the customs counters inside. Unlike the meticulous process in Taipei, the agents passed us through quickly, and we made our way to the outer doorway. Upon leaving the terminal, I was met by a horde of Vietnamese hawkers waving signs for hotels, tours, and other travel options. The clamor was deafening, and I looked around frantically until I spotted a man holding a sign with my name on it. It was Quang, the 37-year-old cyclo driver Opey had recommended to me.

Quang was a skinny, nervous guy who had been a soldier in the Republic of Vietnam's army in the late '80s. His body was slightly stooped, and his eyes shifted when he spoke, as if he were holding something back, or maybe he was just uncomfortable trying to communicate in a foreign language. He'd spent a year fighting the Khmer Rouge in the jungle between Vietnam and Cambodia. He didn't want to talk about it, which was fortunate because his English was pretty limited.

Tan Son Nhat Airport was four miles from Ho Chi Minh City's District 1, the city's business and tourist center. Quang had come in a cab, which he led me to as we elbowed our way through the throng of hawkers. It took us twenty minutes to drive through heavy traffic to the hotel. After we passed through a few open fields, the landscape began filling with ramshackle one- and two-story buildings along increasingly busy streets. The traffic grew heavier with every block, making my stomach lurch with apprehension at the thought of the overwhelmingly huge crowds my travel books had predicted.

One thing that stood out for me was the large number of shoppers I saw through the cab window. After the war the communist government had tried to impose a Marxist economy on the country. When this strategy had failed to fuel growth, the government instituted a market economy in 1986 that allowed for individual enterprise, risk taking, and private ownership. This change ignited the commercial boom sweeping through Vietnam, but the state still imposed rigid control of the news media, elections, religion, and education.

Another thing that struck me was the proportion of motorcycles to conventional automobiles. There were probably ten bikes to every car, and I was amazed to see entire families of four or five scooting along on a single bike, making the machine nearly invisible beneath the stacked bodies. If I didn't look closely, it appeared they were floating down the roadway on their own power. I also noticed the many pedicabs, which were large tricycles with the pedaler's seat elevated in the rear and a passenger seat for three or four people in front. These vehicles were dependable but slow-moving, tending to obstruct traffic as they crawled through the crowded streets.

Eventually we rolled into District 1, where the buildings were taller and the streets wider and more orderly, but even more crowded. Our cab dropped us off at the hotel Quang had chosen, and we entered through the front door. A slightly disheveled man in an unbuttoned, stained shirt asked me to sign the ledger and hand over my passport. I told him I wanted to see the room first, and begrudgingly he led me upstairs to a windowless room the size of an American bathroom. Dusty and dim, it was furnished with a dilapidated chair and bed that looked like they belonged in a garbage bin. I told the hotel owner that I wasn't interested in such a dumpy room, and when he started to argue, I marched down the stairs and out onto the street. Quang followed passively, a hangdog expression creasing his dour face.

Flustered, I had no idea what to do. It was clear that Quang was going to be of no help, so I walked down the block until I spotted a sign for the Sunflower Hotel. Seeing no option, I decided to give it a try. Inside was a tidy foyer leading to a living room set several meters back from the door. Three people were sitting there, and a smiling woman rose to greet us, asking if we wished to rent a room. Her name was Wan, she said, and her family lived on the ground floor and rented the upper three floors to guests. I had been led to expect lodging prices ranging between ten and twenty dollars in District 1—or less, depending on the level of funkiness one could tolerate. There were even dormitories where you could rent a bed for a dollar or less. But with jet lag setting in, I definitely needed something comfortable and orderly. I felt good about this place and asked Wan to show me a room.

She took me to the second floor and opened a bedroom door. The room seemed fine, but I balked when Wan said the rate was twenty-five dollars a night. Though I could afford it, I wanted something more in line with the prices I'd been led to expect. So she led me to the top floor and showed me a brightly colored room priced at eighteen dollars. It was clean, quiet, and spacious, with an air conditioner and a balcony overlooking the street. I immediately accepted.

After I registered for the hotel, I reluctantly surrendered my passport and arranged for Quang to pick me up later for dinner and a tour of the downtown area. After hanging my clothes in the freestanding wardrobe, I stretched out on the bed and attempted to sleep. As tired as I was, however, there was too much adrenaline firing my nervous system to stay down for long. Since it was only midafternoon, I decided to go outside and explore the neighborhood.

The sidewalk was less crowded than what I had seen from the cab, and many of the shops were closed for the afternoon rest period. There were many stores mixed in with hotels, cafés, and buildings that seemed like apartments or private dwellings. Ambling along, I turned a corner and came to a widened sidewalk fronting an official-looking building with a steep flight of stairs where people were sitting several rows deep. Many of them looked at me as I passed by, and a few called out phrases in broken English that I couldn't understand. When I stopped to ask what they were saying, a young girl rose and thrust the baby she had been holding into my arms. Immediately the voices around me rose, and several people began pointing and talking at once, as if telling me that I was now responsible for the infant. Having no idea what any of this meant—or what I was supposed to do with the baby—I started to panic. A few people stood up, and not knowing what was coming next, I hurriedly lay the baby down and walked up the block, ignoring the laughter behind me.

Before reaching the next corner, I passed a young man who whispered intensely as he passed, "Hey, you want young boy, young girl? You tell me, I find." Not breaking my stride, I turned at the next corner and kept walking until I came to a bridge spanning a wide stream. I stopped on the middle of the bridge to regain my composure, and I saw that the houses downstream were much more dilapidated than the ones I'd passed on the street. Some of them had laundry hanging outside, and several had sewage pipes leading from their outer walls into the water. A couple of naked children were splashing waist-deep in the oily, brown, fetid stream.

I crossed the bridge and continued up a winding street to a corner where I thought a left turn would take me back toward my hotel. I made the turn, but the street came to a dead end after two blocks. Reversing my direction, I tried another, but that one curved away from the direction I thought I needed to go. It suddenly occurred to me that I was lost. I realized I'd lost my intention of making only recognizable left and right turns, so I couldn't retrace my steps. I was literally turning in circles to see if I could spot a landmark I recognized from the walk, but there was nothing. I reached into my pocket for my hotel key, groaning because it had no identifying information on it. I'd taken a business card from Wan's hotel, but I had no idea where the address was in relation to my present position. Hearing only Vietnamese spoken around me, I was at a loss for what to do.

At that moment I was nearly run over by a motorcycle racing off the street straight across the sidewalk in front of me. The cycle was driven by a Caucasian guy who stopped outside the open door of a shop where several men were having their hair cut. As he dismounted, I observed that he was a large man, about forty, casually dressed in cut-off shorts and an untucked t-shirt. An old gentleman sitting on a wooden crate handed him some kind of token, but before he could enter the building, I called out to him. "Yo, sir! Hey there!" He turned, showing no impatience at being unexpectedly hailed. I explained that I had just arrived in Saigon, had lost my bearings, and was feeling totally overwhelmed by the unfamiliar surroundings. I showed him the card and asked if he could help me get oriented.

"Righto," he said matter-of-factly, explaining that he was an Australian oil rigger who had been working in Vietnam for a year. "But hold on a minute, mate, and I'll give you a tour myself. Just need to get clipped first. Won't take a minute."

I readily agreed. Leaning against the outer wall of the barber shop, I planted myself next to the old man and noticed that he was guarding a half dozen other motorcycles. The sidewalk and street began filling with more pedestrians as people rose from their afternoon rest. It wasn't long before I was immersed in a combination of diesel fumes, chattering conversations, and the aroma of cooking meat. The traffic was mainly motorcycles and pedicabs, with a few automobiles and an occasional tour bus. The pedestrians were casually dressed in shirts and slacks, with a smattering of sport coats. The exceptions were a few women dressed in *ao dais,* the traditional tunic split up the sides and worn over trousers.

Soon the Aussie returned, introducing himself as David. As he paid the bike guardian and rolled his motorcycle toward the street, we talked a bit. When I shared that I was an American veteran, he eyed my Jungle Jim khakis and smiled cockily.

"Really, mate? Never would have guessed."

His gaze lingered on my Save Tibet cap, and he started to say something but reconsidered, shaking his head and motioning me behind him. With some hesitation, I climbed onto the back of his bike.

"Here we go!" he called over his shoulder, and before I could blink we merged into the heavy traffic. It was at that moment that I remembered how much I hated motorcycles, generally avoiding them with the same fervor with which I avoided eating fire and wrestling alligators. If I were struck or jarred in the wrong way, even a minor accident could seriously damage my arthritic neck and back. Yet at that moment riding on the back of a screaming death machine felt safer than being lost in the frenetic maze of Ho Chi Minh City. So I did the only thing that made sense: I hung on.

David's tour was short but stimulating. Rocketing through a blaze of escalating traffic, we swerved around corners and blasted through intersections past a fleeting assortment of pagodas, museums, government buildings, and statues. At one point he indicated a colossal structure with a doorman in front and yelled over his shoulder, "The Rex Hotel, mate. Where your officers ate pussy and worked out their war games."

Passing another building, which had an American fighter jet sitting inside its iron fence, he screamed, "The commie war museum. All about Uncle Ho."

It all seemed magisterial and elegant, but at that moment, strung out on fatigue, jet lag, and the vastly unfamiliar surroundings, everything was pretty much a blur. Finally, as we spun through a large square, we came to a huge, one-story rectangular building that seemed to encompass several square blocks. The sliding aluminum doors spaced along the front opened and closed continually on streams of people passing in and out. David pulled up before one of the doors and shut off his machine.

"The Ben Tranh market," he announced. "Couldn't let you miss this, mate."

We dismounted and again he accepted a token from an elderly Vietnamese man who was guarding motorcycles parked at the curb. As we approached the door, I was struck by a continuous low-level hum that filled the air. It took a moment before I realized this was simply the collective voice of innumerable conversations taking place inside. The sun was so bright I could see little but milling shadows as I peered in, and we paused for a bit as we entered to let our eyes adjust to the relative dimness under the tin roof. Immediately I was hit by a blast of pungent smells: cilantro, mint, freshly butchered meat, and the accumulated body odor of hordes of shoppers. The cavernous room was the size of an airplane hangar, lit only by fluorescent lights mounted on metal rafters twenty feet above the cement floor.

David nudged me forward and we entered the milling throng. As my vision acclimated, I saw that the entire room was filled with hundreds of tiny booths where people sold everything from silk scarves to pickled squid, from powdered herbs to fancy dresses, bolts of brightly colored cloth, rice cakes, cosmetics, kitchenware, and things I couldn't even identify. Squealing pigs were jammed snout-over-snout in little bamboo cages, as were squirming pink piglets. Across from a stall selling children's clothes, I saw a booth featuring large jars of pickled snakes, brilliantly colored and stacked in coiled layers. The booths were set out in a huge grid encompassing the entire building, crisscrossed by narrow aisles every fifty feet or so.

Walking slowly, we made our way down a side aisle, and David stopped before a corner stand featuring three shelves of finely crafted glassware. "Czechoslovakian glass," he announced. He had to yell to be heard above the clattering din. "Because this is a commie country, they get it duty-free. Hell of a deal if you can get any of it home in one piece."

He paused before the stall, eyeing the two young women proprietors. They looked to be in their mid-twenties, both slender and beautiful, with lustrous black hair streaming down their backs. Each was dressed in a form-fitting blouse and skin-tight jeans. I sensed my guide's easygoing manner shift as he studied the women. He abruptly turned the corner and entered the small inner space, brushing his torso against the younger of the two women. She didn't recoil. David's eyes bore into hers, their bodies nearly touching.

"You like?" she asked, sweeping her hand toward her wares. "You buy? Very cheap. Very beautiful."

"Oh, yes," he said, ignoring the wares but ogling the woman's body as if examining exotic merchandise. "I like very much."

He moved closer to her. "Very beautiful," he crooned, his lips inches from her ear. "Very, very beautiful."

With no warning he reached over her shoulder, again brushing against her body as he retrieved a tall, thin figurine from the shelf—a statue of the Virgin Mary. Holding it at the base with one hand, he stroked its phallic shaft slowly with the other, hooking the young woman's eyes as his hand massaged the narrow tip of the Madonna's head.

"I like very much," he repeated, as he continued to fondle his makeshift penis. "But tell me," he said, "do you like?" She said nothing but again did not recoil.

David set the statue back on the shelf and reached for his wallet. Keeping his eyes locked on the woman's face, he withdrew a fistful of *dong* notes, making sure she saw the large denominations.

His wad of money was probably more than her entire family could make in a year.

"I not buy today, but maybe I come back to buy, yes?" he asked, fingering the bills with the same lewd intensity with which he'd fondled the figurine. Her lips formed a thin smile, but I couldn't tell whether she was encouraging his advance or simply acquiescing to a lost sale.

"You like," she said. "You come back. You buy. Yes?"

"Oh, yes," David answered, pocketing his wallet as he slid his body against hers one last time. "I will come to buy. I promise you. I will come."

"So glad we stopped here, mate," he said as we continued our stroll. "I'm leaving that bird in the bush for now. But she got it right. I will be back."

He looked at me as if expecting a clap on the back. I said nothing.

At the end of the hall, we reached the meat market. More piglets squirmed in bamboo cages, while live chickens clucked within theirs. Slabs of meat and bowls of entrails lined the stalls, as did more types of fish and mollusks than I had ever seen. Several were alive and squirming in a few inches of water. I stood transfixed, observing a woman fishmonger crouching flat-footed as she nursed her baby. With soft cool strokes, she caressed the child's brow, soothing away its troubled frown. As I watched, a stooped, white-haired man approached and uttered a few words to her. Without taking the child from her breast, the woman scooped a live eel from a shallow dish, picked up a large scaling knife, and proceeded to skin the creature alive as it writhed and thrashed in her hands. She wrapped the still twitching eel in newspaper and handed it to the man in exchange for a few crumpled *dong* notes. Shifting her precious cargo to the other breast, she wiped the bloody knife on her trouser leg and stuffed the bills into a tin can at her feet.

"Fucking unbelievable," David whispered, grimacing as he shook his head. "You just haven't seen Vietnam until you've been to a meat market."

We left the market, and David announced that he needed to get back to his apartment to rest up for a party he and a couple of other oil riggers were having with some local women.

"Come along if you'd like," he said. "The girls can always scrounge up another."

I declined, telling him I was married and looking for different kinds of thrills on my journey. A few minutes later, he dropped me off at my hotel with a "Righto, then. Good luck, mate!"

CH 20
MARCH 1, 1996-*Ho Chi Minh City, Vietnam*

At the hotel I trudged up the winding stairway to my room. My mind was reeling from all I'd seen, and feeling overcome by a wave of tiredness, I stretched out on the bed. Before I knew it, there was a knock on my door, and I saw from my watch that it was eight o'clock, the time Quang and I had set for dinner. We were also scheduled to meet Nina, the shop owner Opey had met the year before. He'd given me a card for her, and I wanted to hear about her experiences during the war. "You gotta check her out, man," he'd told me. "Had a son by a Black GI and speaks Number 1 English. Runs a café that's mainly a bar. I think she might have a couple of hookers working out of her back rooms."

There's not much I specifically remember about that night, other than what happened later at Nina's. I do recall climbing into Quang's pedicab and rolling slowly through traffic. Engulfed in an Asian whirlwind of unfamiliar sights and sounds, we stopped for dinner at an outdoor café. I had chicken and vegetables in a stir fry, seasoned with a garlicky cilantro sauce that was unfamiliar but super delicious. Many of the restaurants had charcoal grills filling the air with the sizzling aroma of cooking meat that mixed with the acrid reek of diesel fumes from the motorcycles roaring by. Bikes were everywhere, their piercing whines screaming through the night in meteor showers of shimmering light. The sidewalks were full of people swarming the avenue, eating, shopping, or strolling along in small groups.

After dinner we pedaled slowly through the busy streets as the traffic continued to whiz around us. Quang pointed out a couple of monuments, but it was too dark to see much, and my nerves were starting to get fried from the sensory overload. By ten o'clock I'd had enough, so I told Quang I wanted to visit Nina's before going back to the hotel. He remembered Nina from Opey's visit, and her place of business turned out to be a short ride from where we'd eaten. We parked before a well-lit storefront on a busy block. The store was flanked by a small hotel on one side and what looked like a furniture store on the other. A grocery store a few doors up the street was still doing business, but there were no customers in "Nina's Café."

When we entered, a tall woman about my age greeted us. Nina had a dour expression and flinty, deep-set eyes that asked no questions. She obviously remembered Opey, and when I gave her the card, she opened the envelope to see if it contained anything besides his note. When she saw that it didn't, she barely glanced at the card before putting it down unread. Turning to us, she pointed to a well-stocked bar along one wall and asked, "You want drink?" I ordered a scotch and water and was surprised when she charged me three dollars, about the same price an American bar back home would ask. We made uncomfortable small talk, but Nina appeared uninterested in hearing my story or providing information about her own. She barely responded when I asked her what to see in the city. Intermittently she had phone calls, which she answered in rapid-fire Vietnamese, telling me they were from customers making sure she was open.

At one point her son, whom she called Tom, came by. He was a tall young man, obviously biracial, who had little interest in me after it was clear that Opey had not sent a gift for him. Named after his father, Tom was one of the fifty thousand Amerasian children born from the unions of Vietnamese mothers and American servicemen during the war. Called *bui doi* (dust of life), these children faced ridicule and persecution after the war, and were still considered by many to be less than fully Vietnamese.

Tom soon left and we continued our desultory conversation. A couple of times, different men entered the shop and spoke to Nina, gesturing to a dimly lit area at the back of the shop before leaving. "They come later," Nina told me, pointing in the direction they had indicated. Turning, I noticed three young girls curled up together at the back of the next room, eating off paper plates. They were sprawled out on cushions before a curtained hallway that led to Nina's "back rooms." The girls were in their early teens, and reminded me of little kittens as they ate, arms and legs nearly intertwined, whispering and giggling like young girls anywhere. Naively, I asked Nina if they were related to her. "No, they flowers," she said, explaining matter-of-factly that she was feeding her young prostitutes before the night trade began. I was dumbfounded. The situation could not have been more obvious, but I'd totally missed it. Claire was thirteen at the time, and none of those kids looked much older. I couldn't even imagine my daughter and her friends in that situation, and a wave of nausea swept over me as I stared.

Misreading my interest, Nina asked, "You want flower?"

"Uh, no," I answered, staring at her blankly. "But where do they come from? Where do you get your...flowers?"

Still oblivious to my reaction, Nina answered with casual indifference, as if asked where she bought her scotch. "There," she said, pointing out the front door to the street. "Many flowers, no family. Girl need eat. Come see Nina."

I don't remember any more of that conversation, only that the room seemed smaller, more squalid. Eventually a couple of men entered, and I motioned for Quang that it was time to leave. I'm sure I spoke with Nina before exiting, but I only recall wanting to get the hell out of her shop. As we rode back to my hotel through the thinning traffic, I felt a desperate need to sleep. Quang dropped me off at the hotel, and we agreed that he would pick me up the next morning so I could see more of the city. By the time I slid into bed, it was nearly midnight. I was out moments after my fingers shut off the light.

CH 21

Suddenly I lurched awake, fighting the sheets as if they were on fire. Heart pounding, arms flailing, I knocked the bedside lamp to the floor, then groped the wall for the light switch. Sitting on the bed, I gasped for air as I tried to understand what was happening.

It was 3:00 in the morning. My thoughts were a raging kaleidoscope of dark, looming images—some from the distant past, some from the last twelve hours: dismembered bodies, deformed beggars, babies on sidewalks arms, and legs protruding from the earth, bloody eels writhing. Little girls trapped in the sex trade because they need to eat. It felt like my mind was trying to vomit all it had taken in from this tortured country, but it couldn't find an outlet to discharge the accumulated bile. The panic was more physical than emotional. Every wheezing breath unleashed a wave of pain so excruciating that my lungs felt as if they were being dragged through hot coals. Going back to sleep was out of the question, but staying awake seemed worse. I had the strongest urge to go downstairs, wake up Wan, and tell her to call a doctor, but opening the door felt more frightening than staying barricaded behind it. Drenched in sweat, I tried to do a relaxation exercise, but I couldn't even feel my breath.

For the next two hours, I tried everything I could to relieve the gut-wrenching panic: pacing, praying, writing in my journal, trying more relaxation exercises. Nothing worked. Finally, at the point of exhaustion, I threw myself on the bed and, giving up trying to fight what was happening, I surrendered to what I could not control.

It was at that moment that I remembered the dream.

It had occurred when I was in therapy after the near heroin bust in Mexico. The nightmares of Michael's bloody, pulsating eye were still haunting my sleep, and even though I'd tempered my acting out behavior, I was having startle reactions and highly emotional flashbacks that pretty much dominated my life. In the dream, I was lying on my back in the middle of a small jungle clearing with three elderly Vietnamese men sitting around me. Their demeanor was so calm and loving that I knew they cared for me and were there to support my healing. Suddenly I felt a sharp pain in my right hand. When I looked down, I saw a huge rat gnawing on my palm, chewing into the soft flesh as blood spurted from the wound. The pain was beyond intense, and I recoiled in horror, trying to pull away from the gnashing teeth. But as I did, my body began to spin, spiraling like a windmill within the healing circle. The more my resistance escalated, the faster I spun, and the faster I spun, the more viciously the rat's teeth lacerated my palm.

When I looked to my elders for help, what I saw was anything but comforting. As my panic increased, they began howling with laughter, pointing at me and nearly rolling in the dust as my body writhed and whirled. Every effort I made to escape elicited more hilarious shrieks of laughter that rose in volume as my spinning accelerated. Dumbfounded, I had no idea what was happening but was so exhausted that my resistance began to drop away, and I gave up my effort to escape.

The scene began shifting back and forth. When my reaction to the rat spiked, I spun faster and faster, triggering even greater whoops of laughter from the old men. When I relaxed, their laughter diminished and they resumed their dignified, meditative postures, regarding me again with loving concern. The raging agitation began to settle, and as it did my attention shifted from resisting the rat to maintaining eye contact with the men. As I did so, I was able to surrender into a state of rest, and as my body calmed, the rat also relaxed. There was a gentleness to its touch then, almost a kindness, as it lapped up the blood on my palm, as if cleansing the wound it had inflicted.

This dream was a turning point in my therapy. In understanding that it was not the gnawing rat prolonging the pain, but my frantic effort to escape, my relationship with the inner turmoil began to shift. The emotions were real, I realized, and needed to be directly experienced, not avoided by raging against the military and numbing the pain. Paradoxically, as I allowed myself to feel more deeply, the intensity of the sensations decreased, and until I overwhelmed myself with the veteran PTSD work, my healing continued on a relatively normal course.

In the hotel room in Ho Chi Minh City, I continued to relax the terror driving my reaction. My breathing deepened, and I realized I'd simply had a panic attack, triggered by the experiences of the previous day. A few of my vets had related similar episodes, and although I had never experienced one, panic attacks were a noted symptom of PTSD. Remembering that healing circle of elders and the lesson of the rat, I once again drifted into sleep.

I had no idea at the time, but this dream would reemerge later on my journey.

CH 22
MARCH 2, 1996-*Ho Chi Minh City, Vietnam*

I slept in the next morning, and when I stumbled down the stairs at 11:30, Wan told me Quang had been by earlier and would return soon. He showed up a little after noon, and we set out in his pedicab to get some food and see the sights. The streets were already crowded, so we made slow progress toward the downtown area.

Quang parked at a street corner where a couple of women had set up a huge pot of *pho*, the traditional Vietnamese soup. Along with the aromatic *pho*, they had slender baguettes stuffed with vegetables, meat, and spices. We sat on a couple of low stools the women had put out, and I dug into the delicious food, paying twenty cents for a large bowl of *pho* and a dime for the sandwich.

The women were super friendly and seemed happy to be serving a foreigner, especially one with a long beard. I was starving after the long night, shoveling in the soup with such gusto that I made them laugh. One woman actually spooned extra *pho* into my bowl, telling Quang I was splashing so much on my beard that I wasn't getting enough to eat. They were curious about me and asked Quang where I was from and why I was visiting Vietnam. When he told them that I was an American veteran, they seemed impressed and ladled in more soup. After my depressing experience at Nina's, the ladies' friendliness warmed my heart, giving me hope for my upcoming meetings with the Vietnamese.

Following lunch, we continued our tour. The streets were now even more crowded with bikes, cars, and pedestrians, and I took it all in from the front seat of Quang's pedicab. I was pretty out of it after the panic attack and couldn't muster much interest in particular buildings and landmarks, but I perked up when we came to the Rex Hotel, which David had pointed out to me the day before. Actually, I'd known about the hotel for years and had planned to visit it while in Ho Chi Minh City. As the Aussie had said, the Rex was famous for the fact that American officers had used its magnificent rooftop bar as a gathering place during the war. As such, the hotel was a monument to the Vietnam War as well as to the centuries of Western imperialism that ended with the defeat of the southern Republic of Vietnam in 1975. The building was a stately five-story monolith of two hundred and eighty-six rooms, taking up an entire city block. I told Quang to park in front, saying that I wanted to check out the inside. He seemed unhappy about this, and I knew pedicab drivers were not welcome in the high-end hotels that mainly catered to affluent foreign tourists. Looking at him in his faded shirt and stained trousers, I understood his discomfort. In my khaki jacket and Save Tibet cap, I wasn't decked out much better, but I couldn't have cared less. If the Rex could serve the REMF elite who had directed the war, it could damn sure serve me.

The lobby was spacious and so elegantly furnished that the décor bordered on ostentation, with its massive chandeliers and fake European paintings covering the walls. There were only a couple of people sitting on the overstuffed sofas, and I saw no point in interacting with the front desk, so we quickly made our way to the elevator. I pushed the button for the rooftop bar. Exiting the elevator, we came to a beautiful terrace, and I realized immediately why this was the officers' chosen playground. Unlike the ornate lobby, the sparsely decorated rooftop garden featured an array of lush potted plants that were scattered throughout the sitting area.

The simple décor highlighted both the view of the city and the terrace's beautiful furniture. At one end was a long, elegant bar where a white-haired man in a tuxedo was polishing glasses. There were only a couple of men present, sitting at the bar nursing cocktails. Avoiding them, I wandered through the room, trying to visualize the garden at night. It was easy to imagine the candle-lit tables overlooking city lights, the room full of high-ranking officers knocking back expensive drinks and arguing their war strategies. I paused at the outer railing and regarded the milling traffic below.

Try as I might to appreciate the gorgeous terrace, I could feel only disgust at the contrast between the spit-and-polished REMFs and the grunts. Their experiences couldn't have been more different. The officers' rank allowed them to bask in relative luxury while the rank-and-file infantry had to slog through the tortuous, insect-infested jungle, facing the ever-present threat of getting ambushed. They planned, we fought.

I had intended to have a drink, but resentment evaporated my thirst. I'd seen what I came for, and it was time to leave. Looking for Quang, I found him standing next to the elevator, as if willing himself out of this unfamiliar setting. We hit the "down" button, and I was soon back on the curb, climbing onto Quang's pedicab.

At my request, we stopped at the War Remnants Museum, famous for depicting the horrors of colonial oppression. There was a Huey helicopter exhibited in front of the large building as well as a captured Patton tank and a U.S. bomber that had been shot down. Inside I slowly made my way through the many exhibits. I had been prepared for the anti-American propaganda, but what dominated the displays were not words but simple images: jars of human fetuses deformed by Agent Orange, tiger cages used by the South Vietnamese to torture political prisoners, even a guillotine employed by the French to execute prisoners. The photographic displays showed bodies burned into unrecognizable lumps by napalm, the smoldering aftermath of villages razed by American artillery, photo after photo of children with amputated limbs, men being beaten. They also depicted dozens of dead bodies following the atrocities inflicted on My Lai and other hamlets. I knew the NVA and Viet Cong had also butchered people and destroyed villages (no mention was made of those atrocities in the museum), so I didn't buy the party line on universal Western depravity. Still, there would have been no war without the occupation of the French and the U.S. invasion that followed, and I was sickened at seeing the artifacts and photographic evidence of the suffering endured by the Vietnamese.

I spent a couple of hours in the museum, while Quang had gone outside to wait on his pedicab. My mind was pretty blown away by all I'd seen, and I didn't want to hang out with him and make small talk or see more sights I didn't care about. It was going on late afternoon, so I asked him to take me back to the hotel. Climbing out of the pedicab, I told him that my plans had changed. Waking up that morning, I had realized I was done with the sprawling metropolis of Ho Chi Minh City. Quang seemed disappointed at losing a customer, but I paid him for an extra day and wished him luck. Still exhausted from the previous night, I went to bed early, eagerly anticipating the next stage of my journey.

That morning I'd asked Wan to make me a plane reservation to Da Nang, about four hundred miles up the coast. Lift-off time was early afternoon the next day. After landing in Da Nang, my plan was to take a bus to the small coastal village of Hoi An, seventeen miles south. I'd been advised by Opey and my tour book that Hoi An, a UNESCO World Heritage Site, was a small town with simple beauty and a fascinating history, noted as a haven for the arts (painting, silk screening, sculpture, etc.). It was here, I hoped, that I could find the "New Vietnam" I had come to explore.

CH 23
MARCH 3, 1996–*Plane to Da Nang, Vietnam*

The next afternoon I boarded the plane for Da Nang. Looking forward to seeing the "quaint and artistic historical gem" of Hoi An, I was excited to get on with the journey and meet the Vietnamese in a smaller, more bucolic setting. My spirits soared when the plane rose from the tarmac to begin its eighty-minute flight north. The cabin was only half full, so I had my own row. Edging into the window seat, I dropped my backpack onto the seat next to me to discourage fellow travelers from trying to practice their English on me. I was definitely looking forward to interacting with the folks I was going to meet, but I needed this short respite before starting the next leg of my journey.

I glued myself to the window as we gained altitude, fascinated by the velvety green carpet taking shape below. The forested expanse went on as far as I could see, with a couple of winding rivers cutting through the verdant landscape. From my elevated perch, it appeared soft and almost fluffy, but I knew that was a cruel illusion. My body cringed, remembering the sweltering vegetative horror of the forest floor: the impenetrable stinging brush, ravenous termites and fire ants, leech-filled rivers, poisonous snakes, and scorpions. At times the growth was so dense, the canopy seemed to start at head level and tear at our faces. Nests of ravaging termites regularly fell out of the trees we were crashing through. The ones landing on the neck were the worst—an explosion of carnivorous fury down the shirt, ripping the flesh in dozens of tiny bites. When this happened the grunt immediately threw off his fatigues to get clear of the raging horde, and the entire column halted while the poor guy slapped the slashing attackers off his body and clothes. Once I flicked open a Zippo lighter and held the flame on a branch near a termite. The insect instantly attacked, running down the length of the branch and hurling itself into the flame.

"That is one badass motherfucker," a grunt said, shaking his head.

"As far as I can see," I answered, "they're pretty much *all* badass motherfuckers."

I couldn't deny that the panorama spread out below the plane was gorgeous, but it wasn't a bit tempting. I had no idea what I'd be encountering in the coming days, but revisiting *that* venomous hell was definitely not on my to-do list.

Seeing the jungle also elicited memories of chopper rides, when the Hueys would swarm in to transport us to yet another bunker complex. Six or seven grunts would climb aboard each one. Most of the guys crowded into the interior, grateful for the relative security of being encased within the group. Others, like me, chose to sit facing outward at the edge of the cabin, legs dangling in space, gulping in the welcome blast of air after days of humping through the bristling foliage. I remembered how exhilarating it had been to lie against the seventy-pound rucksack anchoring my back as I perched on the brink of open space, pant legs flapping in the wind. The engine roar was deafening, especially inside, so meeting the whirling air face-on provided a cool, windblown rush that was beyond pleasurable.

The one drawback of that position—along with the possibility of getting thrown out if the chopper pitched—was the distinct disadvantage of coming into a Hot LZ in a position so exposed to enemy fire (a combat delight I thankfully missed in my short tour). The grunts who had been there the longest laughed at me for taking the "hot seat." Unnecessary risks were something one soon learned to avoid in combat, and if I had survived a hot landing, I definitely would have been ragging on the newbies for taking such a foolish risk.

As the flight continued, my mind reeled off more memories. One that stood out was the macabre experience we once had immediately following our landing. It occurred just before Michael's arrival, when we were experiencing a lull in enemy contact. The brass weren't happy about that, so they found something for us to do. In pursuit of the ever-elusive enemy, our company was dropped off near a small village several kilometers from the city of Tay Ninh. The NVA had recently attacked the hamlet, but the army of the Republic of Vietnam had thwarted the strike, killing several NVA soldiers. Once we were on the ground, we entered the jungle and soon arrived at a dirt road on the outskirts of the village. The road led to a cleared area where the enemy bodies had simply been bulldozed into the ground. It was a sight none of us would ever forget: arms and legs protruding from bare earthen mounds like charred branches in the aftermath of a forest fire. Blackened, green-stemmed boots dotted the landscape like dead fruit, while clawed hands reached up to an unseen sky. A momentary silence descended on us as we filed through that strange killing field— bizarre even by *our* standards. We knew the heat of combat all too well, but this was of a different order entirely, and something akin to reverence seemed to come over the company. Any sense of sacredness that may have gotten stirred, however, was quickly broken by excited whoops as the grunts began circling the make-shift burial ground. Before long they were putting lit cigarettes between the rigid gray fingers, posing rakishly as buddies snapped photos of them pretending to shake hands with the dismembered hands.

Along with firefights, it was incidents like this that ultimately shut down my emotions. By the end of the first month, I could mop up the eviscerated intestines of a kid I'd played cards with that afternoon, not wash my hands before dinner, then fall into a dreamless sleep. As I'd discovered on my second night with the company, it didn't matter if the bodies were Vietnamese or American. As the company custodian, my job was to clean them up. I sometimes went days at a time with the blood of two continents caked beneath my fingernails, never missing a beat as I spooned greasy C-rations into my mouth, joking that the bits of gore added spice to the otherwise bland food.

A young flight attendant rescued me from my bitter reverie by announcing our descent into Da Nang, cautioning us to make sure our seatbelts were fastened. I wasn't convinced that a fastened seatbelt would protect me, but I dutifully complied. Relieved to let old memories go, I reminded myself that it was 1996, not 1969, and I was about to begin the next phase of my journey. Raising my seat-back to a level position, I was ready to roll.

CH 24
MARCH 3-10, 1996–*Hoi An, Vietnam*

I was soon walking out of the much smaller Da Nang airport. Pausing at the front door, I scanned the parking lot, looking for the bus that would take me twenty-nine kilometers south to Hoi An. A young airline official approached, sporting a stiff-billed captain's cap and a rumpled white shirt hanging out of blue slacks. Stretching out his right arm, he pointed to the far end of the parking lot where several buses were haphazardly congregated. I hoisted my backpack and followed his finger to the menagerie of vehicles. They were all relics from a bygone era, looking more like rattletraps from *The Grapes of Wrath* than modes of modern transportation. I wound my way through the maze of buses and found the one going to Hoi An. It was so packed with people that they were nearly hanging out the windows. Packages and suitcases of every sort were tied onto the roof, including a box of caged chickens wedged between a wooden chair and a large bamboo basket. I paid the driver for my ticket and wasn't surprised when he said my backpack had to be secured on top.

Climbing on board, I made my way down the aisle, carefully avoiding the feet and smaller packages poking out from both sides. My fellow passengers greeted me, the lone Caucasian, with obvious interest and friendly nods. Most of them were loaded down with parcels and a wide assortment of other items, presumably purchased in Da Nang. There were no available seats in the front, so I had to shuffle my way to the back and squeeze in between a young man and a woman holding a squirming piglet. No one around me could speak more than a few words of English, so after I explained that I was from California and received a few nods of recognition, I pretty much settled into my own world. I stared out the window and enjoyed the ride through the rural countryside.

When we entered Hoi An, the bus pulled alongside a curb on the outskirts of the downtown area. We unwound ourselves from our cramped quarters and slowly filed outside. I secured my backpack and saw that we were in front of the government-run Hoi An Hotel, an imposing, whitewashed structure that my travel book said was the most spacious hotel in town. Remembering my difficulty with the crowded streets of Ho Chi Minh City, space was a commodity I definitely needed, so I decided to check it out.

Passing through an iron gate, I found an immaculately landscaped setting that reminded me more of an English garden than of an Asian hotel. The two cement lions guarding the door would have been as at home in Topeka, Kansas, as in this coastal village in central Vietnam. I entered the building through heavy glass doors that opened to a spacious lobby and a large, white-carpeted sitting room. A long reception desk took up most of the right wall. The entire ground floor teemed with ornate furnishings that seemed ostentatious and out of place. At first glance the room appeared comfortable and plush, but as I took it all in, something definitely felt off. I soon realized it was that the entire place could not have been less Asian. As with the outer grounds, every effort had been made to create a luxurious, high-end décor that would presumably appeal to Western tourists. Massive chandeliers anchored each end of the lobby, and huge upholstered sofas stretched along two walls. A large gilded mirror hung over one sofa and an embroidered French tapestry above the other. The marble floor shone like polished glass. In the middle of the room, a long Baroque table was dominated by an ostentatious silver tea set. Even the two young clerks calling out "Welcome, sir!" from behind the reception desk seemed artificial, a smile stamped onto the face of each fawning young staffer as if it were a company logo.

I thought these trappings were odd for a government-run communist hotel, especially in light of the museum exhibits I'd seen in Ho Chi Minh City depicting the horrors of colonial oppression.

The Socialist Republic of Vietnam had been an independent country for barely twenty years and had been economically shunned by the West since 1975. I understood its need to build an economy, but marketing a colonial motif seemed antithetical to the aim of overcoming colonial oppression. It certainly didn't fit my concept of either the old or the new Vietnam.

In spite of my feelings about the décor, a flood of exhaustion suddenly overtook me, and I realized how overwhelmed I was by all I'd experienced so far on my journey. I paid the smiling staffer twenty-five dollars for my room and made my way toward a hot shower and rest before exploring the town. I headed out around 4:00, and my first impression of Hoi An was that it was quaint, clean, and very friendly. But I was still feeling raw from the Ho Chi Minh City experiences and needed some down time before taking in more stimuli. After exploring a few streets and getting an early dinner, I retreated to my room, wrote in my journal, and sent a letter to Barbara. By 10:00 p.m I was asleep.

The next morning, refreshed and ready to see the city, I spotted a portly fellow tinkering with a motorcycle engine as I exited the hotel. When I walked by, he rose from his work and approached me with a huge smile on his face, arms outstretched as if he were about to give me a hug. He introduced himself as Sgt. Loc, explaining that he had been an ARVN soldier during the war and had worked with the Americans. He assured me that he spoke "much good English" and asked me to hire him to show me the city. Loc's enthusiasm was infectious, and I agreed to hire him. From that moment on, he became my companion and interpreter, steering me through the crowded blur of Vietnam on his motorcycle, explaining Vietnamese customs, and mediating my interactions with the local community.

Sgt. Loc was about my age and, like Major Tony, had spent years in a jungle re-education camp for his "crime" of aiding the Americans. These camps were actually prisons where those who had conspired with the foreign enemy served terms of forced labor and political indoctrination to bring their attitudes in line with Marxist doctrine. Consequently, after his release Loc was not allowed to work in any professional capacity for the rest of his life. His two sons were also excluded from higher education and professional employment, and he later told me how his family had known many lean years following the communist takeover. When Vietnam began opening up to trade and tourism, Loc scraped up the funds to create a small tourist business, driving visitors like me around the countryside and serving the increasingly frequent tour buses passing through Hoi An. His greatest wish, he told me soon after we met, was to make a success of his enterprise in order to help his sons get established in some form of business so they could send their kids to college.

It was with Loc that I discovered the Vietnam I'd been looking for. Hoi An, as it turned out, was the perfect venue for my long overdue introduction to the people the war had estranged me from twenty-seven years earlier. Many of the village residents, inspired by Bill Clinton's termination of economic sanctions, opted to learn English. Nearly everyone I met was thrilled that American tourists were now visiting their country, and they went out of their way to engage me in friendly conversation. When Loc was tending to other tourists, I spent my time wandering the streets and chatting with amiable shop owners. I was dazzled by the beauty of the regional artwork—ceramics, silk apparel, woodcraft, and painting. As a UNESCO World Heritage Site, Hoi An had been a trading hub between Vietnam and the rest of the world for hundreds of years, and the area is rich with architectural wonders built centuries earlier by Portuguese, Dutch, and Japanese traders.

I relaxed for hours at the pristine An Bang Beach just outside of town, then napped or read before enjoying exceptional two-dollar dinners at one of the cafés nestled along the Thu Bon River as it rolled toward the sea. It was an idyllic setting—one that represented the new Vietnam very well, I thought. Clearly the news reports had been correct. For ten days my explorations continued in this vein, with much to explore both in and outside the city. Loc had been born in Hoi An, and he knew the people, the history, and the many back roads. "I will show you many attractions," he promised with a nod and a wink. "I know Americans, and Americans love attractions."

And what amazing attractions there were! Hoi An is located in Quang Nam Province on Vietnam's central coast. The city and surrounding area had been ferociously fought over during the war, and there were many areas familiar to American veterans. Since my tour had been far away and entirely rural, I had no personal memories of the area, but in spite of that I found it fascinating to walk the sands of the famous China Beach, where throngs of American troops had been given short in-country R&Rs. At one point, standing at the far edge of the beach, I could almost see the young men frolicking in the surf, drunk and desperate for a good time, squeezing out every drop of their short respite before heading back to war.

On another occasion Loc drove me to Marble Mountain, which is actually a cluster of five marble and limestone outcroppings that rise from the plain located midway between Hoi An and Da Nang. Each mountain is named after one of the five elements: *Kim*/metal, *Thuy*/water, *Moc*/wood, *Hoa*/fire, *Tho*/earth. All have cave entrances leading to tunnels and staircases that wind upward to huge Buddhist statues carved out of marble. Thuy, the water mountain, is the only one open to tourists, and it was from this entrance that I began my climb.

Loc dropped me off in the tiny village of Dong Hai at the base of Thuy Son, and I was immediately besieged by a group of kids clamoring to be my guide through the inner passages. I chose a quiet boy at the back of the pack, and together we passed through the 400-year-old pagoda of Tam Thai to begin climbing the 156 marble steps and slanted ramps leading to the top of the mountain. We passed several large Buddha figures carved into the side of the passageways, including a reclining Buddha that measured fifty feet long. Eventually we came to the Tam Quan Gate opening and were treated to a magnificent view of the countryside all the way to My Khe Beach and beyond. Continuing upward, we came to a huge cathedral-like hall that I had heard about for years. An American airbase had been constructed next to these mountains during the war, and the Viet Cong had established a large hospital in the upper chamber of Thuy Son. The hospital was literally within earshot of the American base. When I entered that cavernous room, rays of light streamed in from the holes gouged out of the mountaintop by years of American bombing, creating a stunning effect that was as eerie as it was beautiful.

Both my combat experience and my work with the vets had instilled a deep empathy for *everyone* caught up in the war, and as I stood in the dank coolness looking up into the light streams, I could almost hear the echoes of those blasts reverberating throughout the room. Regardless of whose side they were on, my belly lurched, imagining the terror felt by those wounded soldiers decades earlier as the thunderous blasts exploded overhead.

After completing the tour, I was met by a family of sculptors who wanted to show me their artwork. The people in Dong Hai had been sculpting the marble for generations, and a large tented showroom with tables displaying their figurines had been erected near the mountain's entrance. The primary motif was Buddhism, and some pieces had a bluish tint running through the marble that made them breathtakingly beautiful. My funds were limited, and I had to carry whatever I purchased with me, so I needed to be selective. After an hour of browsing, I bought a ten-inch statue of Kwan Yin (the bodhisattva of compassion) and a larger three-figured piece depicting Buddhist fairies. They were both as finely finished as anything I'd seen in American museums. The family's father wrapped my purchases in newspapers and twine, then taped the package into a heavy bag that I carefully placed into my already stuffed backpack.

The days passed serenely as I continued my stay in Hoi An. I roamed the town, exploring the shops and temples and chatting with anyone who cared to talk. One day I met a young man named Ba, who told me he was a school teacher on one of the tiny islets scattered around the mouth of the Thu Bon River. He invited me to visit his school and help celebrate International Women's Day with his fellow teachers. So the following afternoon I boarded a water taxi and made the ten-minute trip to the islet. The school day had just ended, and as the children scurried homeward, Ba came out and ushered me inside.

A group of teachers were seated around a table, drinking warm beer and munching on rice cakes. Except for Ba, none of them spoke English, so I just sat back, sipped my beer, and listened to the men give speeches praising the women in words I didn't understand. The language barrier was actually irrelevant because the sincerity of the men was evident on their faces, and Ba translated much of what was said. The entire group could not have been friendlier, passing me snacks and making sure my glass of beer was full. It was a joy to be accepted with such kindness, and I couldn't help wondering how a lone Vietnamese tourist in America would have been received had the situation been reversed.

On another day I visited a silk shop and placed orders for a shirt for me and kimonos for Barbara and Claire. The family-owned store was filled with bolts of brightly patterned silk, and after making my decision on the colors and discussing sizing, I was told to return in an hour to pick up my purchases. At the appointed time I went back to the shop and retrieved my handsome shirt, which fit perfectly and cost less than two dollars. The kimonos—exquisitely made—cost about four dollars each.

While at the shop, I met the eldest daughter, Bac, a nineteen-year-old who had studied English in the hope of becoming a tourist guide. She offered to show me the outdoor waterfront market, and I accepted. Although I didn't really have a need for her services, given the amount of time Loc was spending with me, I leapt at the chance to chat with a young person who could share what life was like growing up in Vietnam after the war. She had no memory of the conflict, but her early years had been spent in poverty as Vietnam recovered from years of wartime chaos and the Western embargo. I was deeply touched to hear her enthusiastically exclaim how good it was to have hope that her country would know better times in the future. Bac was happy for the opportunity to practice her English and didn't want to charge me for her time. "Oh, no," I said. "You are a professional and need to set a price." This surprised her, and when she couldn't come up with a figure, I said I'd pay her five dollars for the tour. Her eyes lit up as if she'd won the lottery (the average annual income in Vietnam was $400 at the time).

We spent a pleasant hour strolling through the market, and she patiently told me the names of the unfamiliar fruits, vegetables, and spices on display. Although the market was much smaller than the one I'd visited in Ho Chi Minh City, there was still a riot of merchandise—produce, household goods, clothing, artwork, school supplies, and food stands—all engulfed in a medley of pungent odors. Like every market I visited, it also featured jars of colorful dead snakes and a meat market abundant with live eels and caged piglets.

One afternoon Sgt. Loc returned from an excursion he had taken with a busload of Christian vets who were doing a volunteer project at the local orphanage. He was uncharacteristically serious and proceeded to tell me how the bus had been stopped by some young policemen who tried to shake down the vets for money. Since Loc knew these guys were acting on their own rather than carrying out official policy, he refused. An argument ensued and the cops then demanded everyone's passport, which infuriated the vets, who protested loudly and refused the request. Eventually Loc was able to contact a local governmental official, and the order was given to allow the bus to return to Hoi An. When I complimented Loc for his courage in standing up to the policemen, he casually brushed me off, saying the vets were his responsibility. He could not let them be abused by the local militia, who had a reputation for trying to extort illegal "fines" from tourists venturing into the countryside. Knowing that challenging authority in Vietnam was potentially dangerous, I still admired his courage and acceptance of responsibility.

Of all the people I met in Hoi An, one of my favorites was young Oy, who lived in the Catholic orphanage on the edge of town. I met him one afternoon as he was riding his bike past the café where I was drinking coffee. When he saw me sitting outside, he parked the bike and walked over. Looking up, I saw a diminutive, dark-haired boy with wild coal-dust hair exploding over crackling, sunlit eyes and dimples an inch deep. I would have guessed his age to be seven, maybe eight, but later learned that Oy was eleven. Like half of Vietnam's children, his growth had been stunted by disease and malnutrition.

"Hey you!" he nearly shouted. "You American, yes?"

"Yeah," I answered. "I'm American. My name's Bill, what's yours?"

At that moment a look of pure mischief passed through his eyes, and he put his hand on my shoulder. Leaning his face inches from mine, he muttered in a deep, gravelly voice, "Ho Chi Minh."

Clearly this was a kid I wanted to know.

"Nah," I said. "You're too ugly to be Ho Chi Minh. What's your real name?"

He ran away then but soon came back, challenging me to guess his name. I accepted the invitation and started throwing out possibilities. "I'll bet it's George," I said. "Or Henry. Maybe Heathcliff. Wait—it's Archibald, right?"

He looked at me as if I were batshit crazy, too dumbfounded to answer. Finally he shook his head and climbed back on his bike. "Me Oy!" he shouted over his shoulder as he rode down the cobblestone street.

I thought I was done with the little scamp, but he was far from done with me. Oy sought me out as I was having coffee the next morning, asking if I remembered his name.

"Sure," I answered. "You're Archibald." He laughed this time, and that was the start of a memorable relationship I would come to cherish.

Bicycling into town from the orphanage every day, Oy pedaled in and out of my life throughout my stay in Hoi An. He and his bike were a constant presence in the village—careening through the narrow streets, rocketing past shops and temples, scattering pedestrians like bowling pins as proprietors shook their fists at him for creating such a nuisance. As far as I could tell, Oy barely noticed. When he wasn't racing through the streets, he could be found at the silk shop, where Bac and her family let him hang out and run errands. My favorite memory of him came a week later, on the day I visited the village barber.

I had awakened in a funk that morning, full of remorse and bitterness about my damaged relationship with Barbara and Claire. I felt completely isolated in a land where, at best, I was a friendly foreigner. My home life had not been comfortable for some time, but at least it was familiar. Now, as exciting as my time in Hoi An had been, I felt cut off from both continents, vulnerable and alone, too tired to rise, too tired even to sleep. Outside, the teeming masses were coming alive, pouring into the streets for one more day of third-world struggle. In the depth of my fatigue, the mere thought of joining that desperate throng was more painful than anything I could imagine. That day marked a distinct shift in how I related to both my journey and the people I encountered.

Oy found me later that morning at my usual place in the café, but I was in no mood for our usual banter. He ignored my coolness, insisting there was someone he wanted me to meet. I had previously told him I was interested in connecting with soldiers who had fought in the war, and when he told me about the village barber, I sensed that his shop was a place I needed to visit.

"You like Mr. Chien very much," Oy had assured me. "He VC." He then proceeded to give me directions in his typically convoluted language. "Very easy," he said. "You go Nunc Bien Street to third space between shops, go past two wells to house with many chickens, follow road past house with yellow dog. You find big dirt road that go away from village."

In spite of Oy's garbled instructions, I had little trouble finding the barbershop and was surprised to find several men standing outside. Mr. Chien's home was a post-war stuccoed pillbox the size of an American garage, and it soon became apparent that Mr. Chien's front yard *was* the barbershop. A true artist-in-residence, the barber plied his trade in the midst of his customers, having pulled a sun-blistered chair off the front porch announcing that he was open for business that day. Yellow flowers bordered the yard, separating the barbershop from the bustling thoroughfare of Le Loy Avenue. This fragile barricade was the only hedge against the relentless crush of traffic moving to and from the village. Inside the perimeter the men jabbered away in animated conversation, seemingly oblivious to the stream of pedestrians, bikes, motorcycles, and pushcarts that rolled by.

Males of all ages were clustered around the yard—from a tiny, wide-eyed tyke in his father's arms to an elderly gentleman in peasant pajamas squatting flat-footed against the front stoop, head back and dozing. The old man's leathery skin was dark as dirt, his face a mass of jagged, crisscrossed wrinkles. Probably a farmer, I thought.

Before joining the group, I observed the barber's work, fascinated at how different it was from what American barbers offered back home. He was digging wax from ears, giving chiropractic neck adjustments, and shaving the entire faces of his customers with a straightedge razor. Remembering Oy's description of the barber's wartime activity, I couldn't help wincing as I watched his blade slice across so much living flesh. With studious precision, he scraped the forehead, temples, even the bulging surface of the eyes, his left thumb holding each lid firmly in place. He cut along the cheeks, the nose, the lips, down the sides of the mouth and chin, and finally the throat.

Taking a breath, I entered the yard and greeted the men with a hearty *xin cha'o.* Then I bummed a smoke from one of them, using exaggerated hand gestures to communicate my need. As I'd hoped, this elicited a chorus of laughter, and from that moment we began chatting away in a hybrid language none of us really understood. Not counting the old farmer, there were eight customers clustered around the barber's chair, dressed mainly in rumpled slacks and untucked short sleeve shirts. I couldn't follow much of their conversation but sensed their surprise at my presence, even as they made room for me with friendly nods and open-handed gestures. The men were interested in who I was, so I managed to communicate that I was a veteran from California who had served in their country in 1969. That brought exclamations of recognition, especially from those old enough to remember the war years.

I was curious how my information might be received, but the continued friendliness of the group assured me there was no problem. Throughout my journey, I'd found this lack of animosity toward Americans puzzling, considering the extent of death and destruction inflicted on the country. A few days later, on the night before leaving Hoi An, I was to receive an insight into the unique perspective the Vietnamese seem to have on this matter.

Word of my presence had spread, and more and more men filtered in, eyeing me with interest and commenting among themselves. As the volume increased, the old farmer woke with a start. He tumbled off his haunches when he saw me, then quickly regained his footing and rushed forward with an ecstatic toothless grin. Pinching my arm with the bony fingers of one hand, he pointed into the invisible distance with the other, rattling off an excited stream of Vietnamese. I felt certain he was telling me the story of his time with the Americans during the war. Assuming I had come for a haircut, the old man began running his rickety twig fingers over my scalp, meticulously examining the few hairs still planted there (I had removed my Free Tibet cap to wipe off sweat, revealing my baldness). He seemed truly in awe as he exclaimed over and over to his friends at the wonder of it all. Even the war had not prepared him for such a strange occurrence. "Can you imagine?" I understood him to say within the torrent of unintelligible verbiage. "A bald American has come for a haircut!"

I had been there about an hour when Oy found me again. As always, his arrival was a riotous event. One moment I was trying to explain to the men why a bald American needed a haircut, the next we were engulfed in a comet flume of dust as Oy skidded his bicycle across Mr. Chien's nebulous threshold.

"Oh, Missa Bill! Missa Bill!" he wailed from the dust cloud billowing around us. "Bac say you come. Crazy lady make big trouble."

As the dust settled, Oy materialized. Astride his tarnished rust-colored bicycle, he wore the summertime uniform of young boys everywhere: a ragged T-shirt and baggy shorts. One foot was planted solidly in the dust, the other dangled a rubber-soled sandal off the raised pedal. He was in a panic, his entire body vibrating in distress, bursting with the information he had been sent to impart. His elfin face writhed like seawater in a windstorm, lips quivering as he took a deep breath to continue his story of turmoil in the village.

I grasped him gently by the shoulders and locked onto his eyes. "Your English is good, Oy. Very good. But one word at a time. One... word...at...a...time."

He gulped and swallowed, and eventually I learned that an English-speaking tourist was creating a disturbance at the silk shop. Bac had sent Oy to fetch the "friendly foreigner" to help her understand what the woman was saying. I sympathized with Oy, but my relationship with the men had been far too meaningful to end in rudeness on my part. Taking the handlebars in one hand, I lifted the front end of his bike a few inches off the ground, immobilizing my young friend while I continued to shake hands and say my farewell *tam biets*. The air hummed with spirited discussion as the men debated this new turn of events, and I was genuinely sorry to be leaving them with an unanswered question. Why *did* the bald American come for a haircut?

This question was of absolutely no interest to Oy, however. His mission would be incomplete until I had been delivered to Bac, and he was desperate for us to be on our way. Pulling away from my grip, he began rolling his bike back and forth over my toes, nosing the front tire against my knee as he tried to herd me out of the group. Since finding his voice, Oy had not stopped talking.

"We go now, Missa Bill, okay? Hey, Missa Bill, you get on. We go now. Okay? Hey, you!"

We walked Oy's bicycle onto the crowded avenue while the men clustered around us. There seemed to be nothing more to say, so I took the seat and Oy hopped onto the handlebars. As I leaned into the upraised pedal, the old farmer stepped forward and placed his fingers on my wrist. There was no laughter in his eyes then, and he spoke slowly and with great deliberation, punctuating his words with slight squeezes along my arm.

"He say it good you come back," Oy whispered over his shoulder. "He say long time Vietnam have many enemies. Very good you come now as friend."

Taking that as my final gift of the day, I bowed to the elder before me. Then off we rode, merging with the congested traffic as we wove a new seam into the ancient, ever-changing fabric of Vietnam. When we arrived at the silk shop, the emergency had passed. The angry lady—a New Zealander, which made her English difficult for Bac to understand—had mistaken Bac's shop for that of another. When she understood her mistake, Bac had escorted her to her appointed destination. As with my earlier depression, the crisis had been swept away by unforeseen circumstances, and life had been restored to its proper balance.

That night, when I replayed the events of the day, I saw that it was not enough to return to Vietnam simply to meet the people and witness their lives. If I were to be accepted by the Vietnamese at any real level, I had to allow them to tend to *my* need. I had come to the barber shop because I needed to touch familiar ground, to settle back into a psychological soil I knew and could trust. I had come in order to belong.

That was why the bald American came for a haircut.

CH 25
MARCH 10, 1996-*Ha My, Vietnam*

When I had dinner with Loc that evening, I told him of my experience at the barbershop. He was attentive, nodding politely, but it was clear that as a man raised in a society where isolation was virtually nonexistent, he simply couldn't wrap his head around my dilemma. He soon steered the conversation to our outing the next day, telling me he had something he wanted me to see. My visit to Hoi An was coming to an end, and I needed to get to Hue and complete the mission for Johnny in the Imperial City and visit Thich Nhat Hanh's monastery. My plan was to leave in a couple of days, and I wanted to take advantage of the limited time left, so I was anxious to see what Loc had planned.

On the following day we were cruising outside the city on one of the many dirt roads that link the hamlets outside of Hoi An. Suddenly Loc downshifted and started slowing down in an open area. I found this surprising because the entire landscape seemed barren and unpopulated. Stopping near an empty field, he got off the bike and motioned for me to follow. We soon reached a spot where we could see deeper into the field, which sloped upward, and about a hundred meters away I could make out the vague outline of some sort of structure at the hill's crest. Loc simply stared into the distance, saying nothing, which was as unusual for him as it would have been for Oy. He then sighed deeply and proceeded to tell me the sad story of Ha My village.

It happened in February of 1968. A South Korean Marine regiment had been assigned to patrol the area and fight the Viet Cong. On their first inspection of the village, the Korean soldiers were reportedly not hostile to the civilian population, but a few days later a VC mortar attack killed a Korean captain and four soldiers. In retaliation, the South Koreans launched a two-hour artillery attack, dropping 155mm rounds on the village along with extensive machine gun fire from helicopters. Two hundred Korean Marines then swept through the little hamlet, killing every man, woman, and child they could find, raping the women they were about to murder. Before leaving, they dropped napalm rounds, trying to cover up the evidence. Dozens of Vietnamese were killed in the attack, leaving few survivors among the thirty households. The village had remained deserted since that day, the few aging structures in the distance being the only fragments that had escaped the napalm.

This was the first time I had seen Loc so quiet. He stood silently after relating the story. It was clear that he was deeply touched and lost in memory. Eventually he told me that he had known a few men from the Ha My village, some related by marriage to his family. The attack, he said, had greatly intensified the local people's anger and determination to resist the American invaders and their merciless allies. He didn't say it, but I sensed his regret for having contributed to the war through his work with the South Vietnamese Army.

We stayed for only a few minutes more, each locked into our private thoughts and feelings, before Loc said he wanted to leave. I told him how sorry I was that such a thing had happened, and I was glad that Vietnam was now beyond the war and its horror. Loc said nothing, but looked at me with penetrating eyes, as if there were something he wanted to say but couldn't find the words.

We were soon back on the road, winding through rice fields, when we came to one of the many small Buddhist temples dotting the landscape. These pagodas are abundant in Vietnam, usually housing only one or two monks to serve those who live too far from the major monasteries to receive instruction and attend religious ceremonies. We entered the temple grounds and were met by a saffron-robed monk who offered tea and sat with us among a lovely assortment of bonsai trees. He was an elderly man, frail and very kind, speaking his limited reservoir of English so quietly that his words could barely be heard above the twittering of birds in nearby trees. We had been maneuvering contentedly through our language barrier for nearly a half hour when the old monk asked me about my impressions of his country. I immediately started extolling the wondrous progress I had seen, emphasizing how impressed I was that Vietnam had come so far since the war ended in 1975.

"It's so good," I said, "to see your country healthy and well after all she has been through."

On hearing such praise of his country's progress, this previously sedate monk became so agitated and his English so broken that I couldn't understand a word of what he was saying. Finally, with Loc's help, I learned that he wanted me to visit Peace Village, a rural medical clinic just south of Da Nang. His passion was so intense that I quickly agreed. Loc knew of the clinic and assured the monk that he would take me there the next day. With that, we took our leave and arrived back in Hoi An shortly before dinner. My dreams that night were filled with imagined scenes from the Ha My village, but each time I woke, I remembered the clinic I'd be visiting the next day. Vietnam still had many problems, I realized, but wasn't the existence of a medical clinic so close to a small village a hopeful sign? I couldn't wait to find out.

CH 26
MARCH 11, 1996-*Peace Village, Vietnam*

The last thing I packed before leaving Hoi An was Big Harold's silver dollar. I hadn't thought much about it since he gave it to me after our last therapy group, but before heading to Peace Village, I retrieved it from my toiletry bag and slid it into the front pocket of my jeans.

Loc and I set out after lunch, and we were soon whizzing past roadside shops and homes interspersed with rice paddies, ponds, the rare industrial unit, and side roads leading to rural hamlets. Even in Hoi An the crowds are pervasive, rolling in from and out to the countryside like the tide of a great sea. The oppressive mid-day heat discourages most traffic during peak hours, but on that hot afternoon the bustling two-lane roadway was busy with travelers. Some were in cars, many on foot, but most rode motorcycles like ours. I took it all in as we rode, noting how much more congested the road became as we approached Da Nang. The noise of the bike's engine had lulled me into a dreamy stupor, so I jerked in surprise when we suddenly veered right to pass through twin iron gates and saw a spacious green hillside topped by a modest white building. The contrast with the crowded highway could not have been more dramatic. Loc downshifted and we cruised up the long, winding driveway.

Peace Village turned out to be a small single-story building the size of an American ranch house. A plaque beside the front door explained that the clinic had been founded by Le Ly Hayslip, a Vietnamese peasant whose story was told by Oliver Stone in the movie *Heaven & Earth*. Le Ly's rural village had been decimated during the war, and she subsequently married an American engineer who took her to the U.S. A few years later she returned to Vietnam to help bring healing to her battered land by establishing Peace Village as well as an orphanage named the Village of Hope.

As we entered the building, we found ourselves in a small foyer with an open doorway off to one side. As I peered into the room, an elderly gentleman leapt from behind a small wooden desk, knocking over his chair. He had obviously been dozing. Rushing out to greet us, he gripped my hand in both of his, and speaking in rapid-fire Vietnamese, explained that he was the director of the clinic, which had been closed since that morning's session. I was most welcome to stay, he told Loc, and an English-speaking doctor would be back soon. After several handshakes and many bows, the director went back to his desk, and I was left to explore on my own while Loc visited relatives in Da Nang.

Despite our somber experience at Ha My the day before, my mood was light. Hoi An's rural tranquility had provided an oasis of relief after I'd bottomed out in Ho Chi Minh City, and the discovery of a place called Peace Village warmed my heart. Roaming the halls, I assumed the old monk had wanted me to see how Vietnam took care of its people, and I was glad for the opportunity. In this spirit, I marveled again at the new Vietnam as I strolled past a room full of sewing machines used to train women for gainful employment. I turned a corner and discovered a locked medicine cabinet crammed with western pharmaceuticals. I turned another and found a second cabinet filled with indigenous herbs and other native remedies. Wandering past a washroom and kitchen area, I then came to the only closed door I had seen. The director had said to look anywhere I wanted, and since every other door in the clinic had been open, my curiosity was piqued.

The room was dusky. One small rectangular window cast a frail light over the cluttered contents: two large metal fans, scattered boxes of medical supplies, a wooden desk. As my eyes adjusted to the dimness, I also noticed an irregularly shaped pile of...something...at the rear of the room. Sliding my hand along the wall, I switched on the overhead light and was startled to discover a large heap of artificial legs stacked like firewood along the back wall.

The pile was about three feet high, and each limb was made of a thin plastic that was decidedly inferior to the sturdy high-tech prostheses used by some of my vets back home. I did a quick tally and counted fifty legs. All had Vietnamese lettering scribbled along the shin.

For some time I simply stood there, perplexed, wondering why they were there. I finally backed out of the room in search of someone to explain and nearly bumped into the English-speaking doctor the director had mentioned. He was a young Vietnamese man wearing thick black-rimmed eyeglasses and a blue smock. When I asked him about the limbs, the intensity of my question clearly took him by surprise. He grasped my elbow and ushered me into a small conference room, closing the door behind us. Taking a seat, he motioned me with an elaborate hand gesture to sit across from him.

"Mines," he stated simply. The legs were going to villagers who had lost their legs to landmines.

"What?" I exclaimed, somehow not grasping the implication. "Where? How?"

A look of pain twisted the doctor's face. His eyes darted away, shifting their focus to a speck of lint on his smock.

"Mines left from war," he said casually. "All over countryside. Farmer grow food, child run play—boom. Lose leg."

"My God," I whispered, reeling at the thought of this continued maiming more than two decades after the war had ended. "How many people has this happened to?"

His eyes slowly rose to meet mine. "So many," he replied softly. "U-nited Na-tions come look," he carefully enunciated. "Find so many people lose legs."

He scribbled the air with his index finger, trying to compute the problem I had given him. But here the young man's English failed him. For several moments he struggled to convert his reality to the appropriate English numeral.

"Wait," he finally said. He wrote something on a sheet of paper and handed it to me. "This many."

The paper was a sheet of common Vietnamese stationery, thin and roughly textured. On it he had written, *25,000.*

"Twenty-five thousand?" I asked incredulously. "Twenty-five thousand people have lost legs since the war?"

"No, no," he countered, shaking his head emphatically. "Not since war. Now! This many lose legs now."

Snatching back the note, he hunched his entire body over it and spelled out the word *Y-E-A-R*.

"Each year? Twenty-five thousand people lose legs to land-mines each year?"

"Yes." Satisfied that he was finally understood, the doctor's face softened and his hands came to rest on the table between us. The light streaming through the window had faded, leaving a web of flickering shadows on the wall behind him.

I was stunned, and what came out of my mouth next was a question I have come to regret. "But what...? I mean who...?"

He leaned into the space separating us, spreading his fingers as if releasing the only relevant answer. "Child not care who. Farmer not care who."

The late-afternoon shadows deepened as we lapsed into a meditative silence. But the quietness only intensified the question in my eyes, and finally the doctor spoke again, in a tone devoid of the slightest inflection.

"Soldiers put mines," he said. "Soldiers all sides." Gesturing toward the window, he added, "All over countryside."

"Does anyone know how many?"

"Yes, yes." He reached again for the paper and pen, furiously scratching out his first attempt before completing the figure he held up for me to see: *3,500,000.*

"Three-and-a-half million?" I gasped. "There are still three-and-a-half million landmines buried in the countryside?"

"Yes."

Oddly, the serious young man smiled, then flicked the end of his pen toward me as if rewarding a plodding student for the right answer. "U-nited Na-tions say."

A wave of terrifying realization suddenly swept over me, and I found myself struggling to grasp the implication of what I had just heard. "But then...the war...it isn't really over," I stammered. "The war is still going on."

"Of course," he sighed, shrugging his shoulders in the resigned manner I had come to recognize as being very Vietnamese. "War always go on."

He reached again for the paper, shaking his head slowly as he studied the numbers. "War always go on," he repeated. Shrugging again, he crumpled the paper and tossed it into a wastebasket near the door.

The young doctor then pushed back his chair, rose, and met my eyes one last time before returning to the job at hand. "So many more to lose."

On the way out, the medical director showed me reports in English verifying Agent Orange had caused one million birth defects in the civilian population.

Sgt. Loc arrived a short time later, and we were soon on our way back to my hotel in Hoi An. My friend had been curiously non-responsive when I told him what I had seen. Crouching flat-footed as he tinkered with a screwdriver inside his motorcycle's guts, he seemed more intent on the journey home than on hearing about my strange discovery, letting me know through an impassive grunt that landmines are a part of life in the new Vietnam as well as in the old. "Mines, yeah, yeah. Legs? Sure, legs. Okay, we go now."

He dropped me at my hotel and we agreed to meet for dinner a few hours later. Loc roared off, and I walked across the large open lobby calling out my usual greetings to the smiling young staffers behind the desk. Remembering their stories of rural village life before moving to the "big city" of Hoi An, I wondered if *those* fields covered waiting landmines. It felt good to be off the motorcycle, but my body was still humming from both the ride and what I'd learned at the clinic. Too restless to go to my room, I plopped down on one of the overstuffed armchairs to let it all settle in.

My experience at Peace Village had brought anything but peace. The young doctor's revelations had shaken me, and as I cast my gaze about the room's ornate furnishings, I was struck by the discrepancy between the hotel's pristine environment (which seemed to epitomize the new Vietnam very nicely) and the hidden minefields of the countryside. A flood of exhaustion suddenly overtook me, and I realized how impacted I was by what I'd seen and heard. Rising from the chair, I made my way to my room, looking forward to a hot shower and rest before dinner.

CH 27
MARCH 11, 1996-*Hoi An café, Vietnam*

Back in the hotel, I was soon pacing my room from wall to wall. The image of all those legs kept swirling in my mind. I tried to ease the tension by writing in my journal and sending a postcard to Barbara, but the images kept coming, and I found myself marveling at what a multifaceted mystery this new Vietnam was turning out to be. The more I thought about it, the more those hidden landmines seemed the perfect metaphor for the underbelly of a country that may not have changed so much after all.

The newly acquired opportunities were available to relatively few, I realized. In my rush to find Vietnam recovering from the war, I'd passed over so much, dazzled as I was by the bustling optimism of those I met. Did the new Vietnam represent true progress, I wondered, or was it—like the colonial façade of the hotel—simply a marketing strategy designed to lure tourism and industry into the country?

Discovering the artificial legs at Peace Village confronted me with a paradox that exposed my naive preconceptions. A peace treaty supposedly ends a war, but what value is an alleged peace that maims 25,000 people a year and continues to sicken people years after the hostilities have ended? Under these conditions, what is even meant by the term peace?

The most baffling mystery, however, was the extreme friendliness with which I—a returning invader—was received in Vietnam. There are varying accounts of just how many Vietnamese had died in the American phase of the country's protracted war with the West. Estimates hover around a million fatalities, with noncombatants comprising thirty to forty percent of the casualties. Add to that the continuing carnage of dormant landmines, Agent Orange, and two decades of enforced poverty, and there is ample cause for ongoing hatred. But with few exceptions, the Vietnamese had greeted me like a long-lost family member.

Forgiveness in the face of ongoing anguish is a lofty goal. From the perspective of American veterans I'd treated, the release of anger toward all who had contributed to their traumatic experiences—the enemy, U.S. politicians, military leaders, and the American people who blamed the warriors for the war—is a core aspect of the healing process. Because the diversity of experience among American veterans is so great and because Western thought focuses on personal healing rather than on the collective, their issues must be dealt with on a personal basis, according to individual circumstance. But the Vietnamese seem to have arrived at this level of acceptance en masse. Finding this to be remarkable, I wondered if their ability to transcend the past was due to a specific cultural trait, perhaps the country's Buddhist tradition.

Later that night I asked Loc why the Vietnamese people seemed to feel no animosity toward their old enemies. It was about ten o'clock. We had just finished our dinner and were drinking beer by the open window of a small café. Comfortably ensconced on a wooden porch elevated a few feet above Bach Dang Street on the Thu Bon River, we were surrounded by the aroma of cooking meat. A large party of Vietnamese men had taken several of the inside tables, their raucous laughter filling the air as densely as the smoke pouring off the charcoal grill. I could see them through the window, hoisting their glasses above the tables strung together to accommodate their party. After my visit to Peace Village, it seemed inconceivable that anyone could be so carefree with three and a half million landmines in their midst.

I looked at Loc, remembering the story of his four-year imprisonment for aiding the Americans. I realized that the question I was about to ask pertained to our personal relationship as well as to his people's attitude toward mine. "How is it," I asked, "that the Vietnamese can be so warm toward those who brought such devastation to their country? That they seem so able to forgive?"

He paused before replying, drumming his fingertips on the table. The bellowing of the men had momentarily subsided. Bach Dang Street was nearly empty, its cobblestone surface winding peacefully along the river as it fell toward the sea. A rare stillness drifted over us, and I pondered my question of forgiveness as Loc pursued his thoughts. The silence was broken when Loc called out to the café owner, a stooped old woman in black trousers and stained cotton shirt who stood just inside the doorway. She came toward us slowly, shuffling onto the porch, a small tray in one hand and a rag in the other. She paused when she got to our table, and in spite of her frail appearance, she emanated an air of great strength as she stood above us. Her white-streaked hair was pulled off her face into a tight bun, highlighting a sun-charred face that was a spider web of wrinkles and pits. Betel nut-stained teeth darkened her weary, quizzical smile, set below eyes as impenetrable as granite. Loc spoke to her in Vietnamese, and her smile faded as she regarded me out of the corner of her eyes while he explained my question. When he finished, she set down her tray, drew up a chair, and sat at the head of our small table. She remained silent for several moments, her gaze lowered as if staring into herself. Her eyes finally rose to meet mine. Leaning one arm on the table, she pointed backward—to the north—with the other. As she began her tale, the sights and sounds of the café melted away. Loc began translating in a soft whisper.

"She born far from here," Loc said, "in small village where Ho Chi Minh Trail come to Vietnam from Laos. All her family killed in the war. All."

First they were caught in the crossfire between the North Vietnamese Army and government soldiers as they battled for control of her rural province. Then they were the victims of American bombs. Her parents were among the first to die, leaving her an only child. She watched as her grandparents, aunts, uncles, and cousins disappeared and the tiny community collapsed. Ultimately she was sent to a Catholic orphanage in Da Nang.

"I am the only one in my family who survived," she said in Vietnamese, her voice clear and even, as if stating a simple fact. Her eyes caught fire when she saw my sad expression in response to Loc's translation. Cutting the air with her palm, she raised a single finger. The only one!

I was speechless and oddly numb, considering the depth of what had just been shared. For one long moment, the silence lingered uneasily in the cool night air, the roar of her loss bellowing in my ears. A barefoot toddler suddenly emerged from the restaurant doorway, staring solemnly at our little group as she sucked her thumb. Catching my eye, she whirled around and scampered back inside. As the child disappeared, the suffering of this woman and her hamlet welled up inside me like a geyser about to explode. For no reason other than to alleviate my screaming discomfort, I touched her hand and said the only words that seemed even remotely appropriate.

"I am so very sorry."

She jerked away, her face twisting into a puzzled grimace. And then, surprisingly, she spoke to me in English.

"Why you sorry?" she asked. "Is not you. You no do this. Is war. War kill people."

Once again I had no reply. She began to swab absently at the plastic tablecloth, and it was obvious that my reaching out to her had interrupted her story. She looked uncertainly at Loc before continuing in Vietnamese. The war was in the past, she said, and Vietnam was moving toward a future that held little time for mourning and regrets. She had children now, and they had children. Her bloodline would continue. I opened my mouth to speak, but she waved me off. She was the first of a new line, she stated proudly, pointing fiercely to her chest. The first!

We sat quietly for several minutes. The street was now completely deserted, and for the first time since we'd arrived, I could hear the velvety whisper of the river. Our hostess had withdrawn into herself, and I could sense Loc eyeing me with interest as I digested her story. She eventually rose to resume her work, speaking directly to Loc as she reclaimed her tray, indicating through a hand gesture that the message was meant for me.

"She say Americans no feel bad," Loc translated. "Come be friends with Vietnamese."

"Please tell them to come," the café owner said as she cleared away our bottles. "Tell the Americans to come."

Her tale had pierced my heart, and I struggled to contain a flood of emotions I knew would not be welcome. Taking a deep breath, I reached into the pocket of my jeans for a handkerchief. And it was at that moment that my fingers touched something flat and hard—Big Harold's silver dollar. I drew it out and offered it to her, extending my open palm in a gift-giving gesture. She regarded the coin with obvious puzzlement, making no move to claim it. Her hesitation made me realize that, while she undoubtedly had seen many American greenbacks, this was likely the first such coin she had encountered. Finally she reached out with her thumb and index finger and carefully took it from my hand, holding it in both of hers as she suspiciously examined both sides. She slowly lifted the coin to her mouth and bit down hard, wiggling it between her teeth. Removing it, she held it at arm's length and shrugged, still clearly unsure whether it was something of value or simply a metal trinket.

I sensed she was about to leave, but I still wasn't sure how her story answered my question about forgiveness. Wanting to prolong the moment, I blurted the first thing that came to mind.

Loc started to translate, but she immediately interrupted.

"Ho," the woman spat out a rush of Vietnamese that caused Loc to rock back in his chair, laughing. Startled, I looked at my friend, waiting for him to translate.

"She say French the language of passion," he chuckled, "and passion only thing Vietnam have too much many years. But English," he continued with a sweep of his arm and a sober wink, "English is language of commerce."

Leaning forward, Sgt. Loc smiled gravely as he handed me the café bill. "We want *commerce*."

The emphasis he put on that word was so sharp, it felt like a slap in the face. I immediately realized that his intensity conveyed not only the extent of his people's wartime suffering, but also the years of suffering from landmines, Agent Orange, and the economic devastation imposed by the American embargo. After hearing the café owner's story, I never again underestimated the inconceivable damage done to this beleaguered country, or the many hurdles she still had to face.

CH 28
MARCH 12, 1996-*Lang Co, Vietnam*

That was my last day in Hoi An. I'd arranged for Loc to drive me north to the next leg of my journey, the coastal village of Lang Co. My plan was to rest there overnight and find a ride the next day for the 60-kilometer drive to Hue. As exhilarating as the trip had been thus far, I still wasn't getting any insight about dealing with my family crisis. I was hoping a change of scenery and new experiences would provide some clarity on how I could rekindle the loving connections we had known prior to my work with the vets. Hoi An had given me much needed grounding since the panic attack in Ho Chi Minh City, and Loc had proven to be a true comrade as he drove me throughout the countryside. It had been a remarkable ten-day adventure meeting the people the war had estranged me from in 1969. Now it was time to move on. But there was one more stop I needed to make in Da Nang.

Prior to leaving for Vietnam the year before, Opey had asked if there was anything I wanted him to do in my name while he was there. This was something I hadn't considered, and nothing came to me for a few days. But as I was getting ready for bed one night, the answer suddenly came to me. I had been awarded the Silver Star for my actions on the day I got hit. Initially I was proud of the recognition, but later, with endless time on my hands in the hospital, I did a lot of research on U.S. foreign policy that changed my attitude dramatically.

As disgusted as I was with the war, I had still believed at the time that we were fighting for a noble cause. I soon realized that defending the puppet government in Saigon was a sham—and anything but noble. The more I read, the more the purpose of the war became clear. After Vietnam defeated France in 1954, retaining control of the country was simply a vestige of centuries-old Western imperialism. The goal was to maintain corrupt, outdated colonial rule by conquering undeveloped countries and utilizing their resources in the interest of the conquerors and their corporations.

I was proud that I'd risked my life to get that grunt out of the clearing, but receiving a medal for participating in an immoral invasion I no longer believed in felt like the ultimate hypocrisy. I refused to attend the award ceremony and instructed the hospital clerk to mail the medal home to my parents. That had been a difficult decision to make. Attending the ceremony would have meant so much to my dad, and seeing the pride in his eyes would have fulfilled the commitment I'd made on his behalf in childhood. But it was a matter of personal integrity, and I had seen way too much suffering on all sides to continue justifying a war that should never have been fought in the first place. My opposition to the Vietnam War created a painful chasm in my relationship with the Old Man, but we reconciled a few years before his death in 1976. We never saw eye to eye on U.S. foreign policy, but we came to realize that filial love far outweighed political bias.

My mother sent me the medal after my dad died, and I had stashed it in my garage without a second thought. When Opey asked what he might do for me in Vietnam, I suddenly realized I could give my Silver Star a renewed purpose. I asked him to find someone who had suffered greatly in the war, and to present my medal to him or her with my apologies. While in Da Nang, Opey met Mr. Duong, the director of a small local school. Like the café owner, he had lost both parents and his siblings in the Tet Offensive when he was very young, and he consequently grew up in an orphanage. Years later he opened the school to provide the education to others that his deceased siblings had never received. Opey reported back that my Silver Star was now hanging in the school's display case. Now, for whatever reason, I wanted to see it one last time.

Loc navigated the usual glut of traffic and found the small whitewashed building with little trouble. We spent an hour talking with Mr. Duong and enjoying a delicious lunch of roasted chicken and vegetables. He showed me the medal, which hung in a display case near the school's front door. I couldn't help thinking that anyone who saw it would have no more understanding of its meaning than the café owner had had about Big Harold's silver dollar. But that didn't seem to matter at all, and I felt at peace knowing that it rested in the land that had gone through so much to defend its freedom.

After saying goodbye to Mr. Duong, Loc and I climbed back on the bike and continued our journey. This involved a 21-kilometer ride over the infamous Hai Van Pass with its hairpin turns, expansive vistas, and deep chasms. Nicknamed the Ocean Cloud Pass because of the heavy mist that often obscures visibility around its tortuous curves, Hai Van is a 1,627-foot-high obstacle course that has been the scene of innumerable fatal crashes over many decades. Loc had mentioned this earlier, reminding me that he was an excellent driver and there was no cause to worry. But then, I was the guy who hated motorcycles, so my stomach plunged every time we lurched around a blind curve. My apprehension was not helped by seeing so many Buddhist shrines memorializing loved ones who had been killed along the way. Since I was there, a four-mile-long tunnel has been constructed, eliminating the treacherous drop-offs and making the road much safer. But in 1996 it was all open road and treacherous chasms.

Descending into Lang Co, we passed through the fishing village at Lang Co Bay and drove through town on Highway 1. We rode past shops, homes, a café, and a small brick-making factory where workers were laying out their rough clay products to dry in the sun. Other than the bay and the estuary, the town seemed small and rather drab. At the edge of the village, we came to a single-story state-run hotel. Loc headed up a short driveway to the front office, where I registered for one of the rooms in back, facing the ocean.

After I dropped off my pack in the room, I met Loc in the parking lot to say good-bye. He had transformed my experience of

Vietnam, and I was sad at the thought of continuing my journey without him. We walked to his motorcycle, and I asked him how much I owed him for the ride to Lang Co, but he just shook his head.

"No problem," he said. "No problem."

I thought of stuffing some bills into his shirt pocket, but I realized he was offering the ride as a gift, so I thanked him and told him how much I appreciated our time together and all he had done for me. I saw tears in his eyes as we shook hands, telling each other to take care as we went off on our respective journeys. Watching him descend the long driveway, I was grateful for having made such a friend.

The hotel sat on the crest of a sand dune overlooking the South China Sea, fifty meters away. It was midafternoon, the grounds were deserted and the beach was empty for as far as I could see. After the continuous interaction in Hoi An, the spaciousness felt luxurious, so I took a long walk on the beach and let the waves lap softly at my feet. The air was so clear and the surrounding silence so comforting that I stopped, closed my eyes, and simply breathed in the experience before heading back to my room.

Halfway there I was accosted by a bunch of screaming kids, accompanied by a woman strolling behind them. They descended on me in a pack, attempting to sell a variety of goods—seashells, cheap trinkets, pastries, warm bottles of Coca-Cola.

"No, no!" I yelled. "No buy."

But they kept coming at me like a mob of chattering monkeys—first one, then another, then two or three at a time. They blocked my way, surrounding me as they shoved their wares in my face. There seemed no way to escape. When I changed direction, they followed. When I sat down, they created a semicircle around me, jabbering incessantly.

"You buy, mister, you buy."

If I made even the slightest eye contact, it elicited more cries. Finally I started trotting up the sand bank toward my room in an attempt to get away. The little peddlers followed, nipping at my heels. As I was running, I noticed the woman who had arrived with the children sitting by herself in the sand. I stopped and asked her to please make the kids stop harassing me. I gesticulated wildly to make my point, not sure if she would understand. She said nothing but beamed in a way I can only describe as beatific. Her eyes were warm, and the wisp of a tender smile played on her face. She invited me to join her with a small hand gesture, then dismissed the kids with a warm smile and wave of her hand. They moved off but stayed close by, forming a little group squatting flat-footed in the sand. The woman was about forty, simply dressed in baggy cotton trousers and a faded blouse. Her straight black hair fell halfway down her back. Although her eyes shone with energy, her body was so still it seemed anchored in the sand.

I accepted her offer and sat beside her. Ordinarily, I wouldn't have placed myself so close to an unknown woman, but her warmth and serenity drew me to her. I hadn't been aware she was singing, but immediately I became absorbed in her soft lyrical hum, so poignant it sent shivers down my spine. I don't remember words, and maybe there weren't any, but the humming was a song in itself, the notes rising and falling in waves of unbearable sadness, evoking her people's age-old struggle to survive in a world that guarantees only suffering and loss. Her voice was clear and resonant, its lilting vibrato expressing both the heartache of life and the enduring perseverance that has sustained the Vietnamese people through centuries of war, pestilence, and famine.

She paused after a few minutes and asked me in faltering English to forgive the kids because they needed to make money to help support their families. There was little source of income in the village, she said, and many of the men were unable to find gainful employment. I told her that her singing soothed my heart, and I'd love to hear more. I handed her a large *dong* note and said it was for her children, then asked her to continue the lovely melody. She thanked me and resumed the song, smiling and turning her attention back to the sea.

At one point she paused again and touched my pale forearm. "Beautiful," she said, drawing out the word in three syllables. "Like sun." She touched her own arm. "Ugly, like dirt." The smile didn't waver, but her eyes seemed as sad as her melancholic song.

I was speechless, but quickly recovered. Taking her hand, I exclaimed, "No, no. Your skin is brown and alive, so beautiful." My hand was resting on hers, and I touched the back of my palm. "Mine is white, like a ghost. No color."

She regarded me calmly, as if placating a blubbering child. There were no words, but her steady gaze made me remember that light skin is a symbol of aristocracy in Asia—the mark of people who didn't have to work in the blistering sun to make a living. Privileged people. People like me.

My companion began humming again, and we spent another fifteen minutes sitting in the afternoon breeze, listening to the gentle waves dancing with the bittersweet notes of her song. Eventually she rose and said she must return home and make dinner. I thanked her again, and her eyes lingered on mine for just a few seconds. Then she was gone. I rested there for a few minutes, letting sand run through my fingers and feeling the echo of something I couldn't quite identify.

Heading toward my room, I paused to give my remaining *dong* notes to the kids (my money belt was stored in the hotel safe). The money I gave them was about thirty bucks, but in a land where the average annual income was $400, it was an unexpected windfall to the five kids. They took the cash with startled eyes and grabby little fingers. Then, with barely a hiccup, they started shoving their stuff at me again.

"You buy, mister, you buy."

Realizing they lived in a world I'd never known, I just shrugged and continued on. Nearing my room, I nearly tripped over one of the kids who was rushing to get ahead of me. At that moment a Vietnamese man came over the hill, and the children immediately hung back. The man ignored them, and I was impressed that his mere presence had that effect on the aggressive little beggars. But I also noticed they seemed afraid, shrinking away from the guy, glancing furtively at one another. Clearly the fellow wanted to communicate with me but could speak only a smattering of English. He looked to be in his mid-forties, short even by Vietnamese standards, and was trying overly hard to be friendly. His eyes were intense and a tad shifty, meeting mine for only a moment at a time, the smile too wide, the speech too fast. Even so, I came to understand his name was Quang and he was the husband of the woman on the beach and father to a couple of the kids. We chatted for a bit, then he told me he'd come back after dinner to talk some more. He said this as he turned away, ending the conversation.

Later, while attempting to rest in my room, I was startled by a deafening mechanical roar outside my window. I stepped outside to see a lone rider on a huge Harley Davidson, pulling up to a room a few doors down. The man removed his helmet while still straddling the bike, releasing a mass of unruly blond hair. Catching my eye, he broke into a huge grin and waved, yelling "Hi, neighbor!" in an accent I soon learned was Swedish. I gave a weak wave as the guy climbed off his bike, unloaded his gear, and disappeared behind the door to his room. I was not ready for this. After my mind-blowing experiences at Peace Village and at the café, I was basking in the reprieve from sensory input and looking forward to some quiet time. But I suspected that was not to be, and it turned out that my neighbor's arrival was the harbinger of what was to become a long and interesting night.

A half hour later he was back at his bike, so I walked out to meet him. Anders was a freelance photographer, riding from Hanoi to Ho Chi Minh City to take photos of the Vietnam coast for *National Geographic*. He was a tall, angular guy with a fair complexion and the ultra-light hair so distinctive of the Swedish stereotype. He was middle-aged and super friendly, seeming to need human contact after traveling alone for several days. I was okay chatting with him for a bit, but I really wanted to retreat back to my solitude. He was telling me about his experiences on the road when we heard muffled voices and shuffling feet coming up the driveway. Four young people rounded the corner to the rooms, three young men and a woman. They appeared to be in their early- to mid-20s, and I recognized that they were speaking French. As with Anders, their English was excellent, and I soon realized that my brief taste of silence and space was at an end.

We talked for a bit, comparing notes on where we had been and sharing experiences. They had taken two rooms, one for the girl and her boyfriend and one for the other two. We all needed to take a break, but the French girl suggested we go for dinner later at the small restaurant across from the hotel's front office. I returned to my room and managed to doze for a while. A tap on my door around seven o'clock got me to my feet, and my growling stomach told me I was definitely ready to eat. It was a short walk to the restaurant, which was actually a side room in the family's house. The only customers in the place, we sat at a large table and ordered beer. The menu featured only one item: baked fish in a spicy plum sauce that turned out to be delicious. The conversation was pleasant enough, but while Anders loved meeting the locals whose photos he took, the French kids spoke only of where they had gone and had nothing good to say about the Vietnamese, whom they considered backward and rather primitive.

We were back on the sidewalk between our rooms when Anders suggested we gather some driftwood and build a fire on the beach. We all thought that was a great idea, but before we could act on it, we saw a lone figure slowly ambling up the driveway. As the figure came into the dim light, we saw that it was a young Asian man who didn't appear to be Vietnamese. He introduced himself as Yoji, a Japanese medical student who was using his short school vacation to explore the coast of central Vietnam. His English was marginal at best, but he managed to communicate that he'd flown into Ho Chi Minh City a week earlier. There he'd scored a large bag of marijuana to keep him as loaded as possible on his vacation. So far he had met his goal, he said, and now he had one week left before his reporting date at school. This new development put the beach fire idea on pause, since everyone wanted to help Yoji continue to achieve his goal. Consequently, after he dropped off his backpack in his room, we all gathered at one end of the walkway and began passing around one joint after another.

It had been several years since I'd used cannabis, but since I was in Vietnam for new experiences, I decided to go with the flow. As our merry little band got stoned, the conversation grew more and more animated. To add to the mood, I retrieved a bottle of Johnny Walker Black Label whisky from my room—an impulse buy from Hoi An. The taste was sharp, acrid, and wretched. I later learned that shopkeepers routinely emptied out the scotch and replaced it with homegrown moonshine. The difference was obvious at first sip. Of course we drank it anyway, sitting in a semicircle on the walkway and laughing up a storm, rambling on about things none of us would remember in the morning. Every once in a while, someone would note the absence of a joint and request that Yoji fire one up. Each time that happened, Yoji would brighten up and exclaim, "Why not?"—the one English phrase he had down pat. Beaming brightly, he'd fire up another reefer, and around the circle it went. The poor guy could barely follow the conversation, yet he seemed totally content at having found a group so supportive of his vacation plan. The booze kicked up our frivolity a notch, and at one point I saw that Quang had joined us and was pulling harder than most at the bottle. I don't remember much else about that evening because that's what happens in such circumstances, but we eventually did make our way to the beach and started a massive bonfire that sent a cascade of flaming sparks into the night.

I was intent on getting on my way before noon the next day, so I laid off the booze and cannabis at around eleven o'clock and headed for bed. On the veranda I noticed that the whisky was gone. The bottle had been about half full when we walked to the sand, and I remembered that Quang was the last one to hoist it before he'd disappeared when we started the fire. Briefly I wondered where he was but soon realized I didn't care. Feeling woozy from the excessive substance intake, I made it to my room and slept fitfully through the night.

I pulled myself out of bed around eight o'clock the next morning and went alone to the café for a breakfast of eggs and a baguette. The food settled my stomach, and three cups of strong coffee eased my hangover, making me feel better than I'd expected. My plan for the day was to head north to Hue, and the hotel manager had arranged for his son Ngo to take me there on his motorcycle. (I can't say I was getting over my fear of motorcycles, but I was certainly getting accustomed to the experience.) Since I had an hour to kill while waiting for Ngo, I perused my tour books, rereading about what happened in Hue during the first Tet Offensive in 1968. When Ngo showed up, I was packed and ready to roll.

As I climbed on the bike, a young boy, whom I recognized as one of the beach urchins, approached me. He motioned for me to listen, and I bent down so I could hear his low whisper. Speaking better English than I would have imagined, he begged me not to give his father any more whisky because it made him mean. Apparently Quang had beaten the boy's mother after returning home the previous night. The child pantomimed a blow to the eye with his little fist, and I understood that the lovely singer had been the victim of some serious spousal abuse.

The news sickened me, and I had no idea what to do. My driver was gunning his bike because a light rain was starting and he wanted to get going before the weather worsened. Caught in a whirlwind of emotion, I handed the little boy more *dong* notes for his mother and told him I was so sorry. Then, as we started rolling down the driveway, I called out my final *tam biets* to my companions of the night before, and off we went.

CH 29
MARCH 13, 1996–*Hue, Vietnam*

The rain picked up a few minutes after we left, and Ngo pulled over to remove two plastic ponchos from his saddlebag. While the poncho shielded my body, it didn't do much to protect my face, so I drew the hood cord as tightly as possible, exposing only my nose and eyes. Even so, my vision was so blurred I could barely see three feet ahead of the bike. Ngo, like most Vietnamese I met, wanted to practice his English as we drove, so we started yelling back and forth as we sped along. The sound of the rain drowned out our voices, though, and we soon had to give it up and just plow through the sixty kilometers to Hue.

I was glad we couldn't talk because hearing that Quang had beaten his wife sent waves of shame and sorrow coursing through my nervous system. Visualizing her kind eyes getting smashed with a fist made my entire body cringe, because I knew it was *my* bottle that had fueled his rage. Even though I hadn't known he was a violent alcoholic, I had seen the kids' reaction to him and should have registered that alcohol was potentially dangerous for such a man. It was also clear that my trouble at home had roots in my heavy weekend drinking that only masked the anxiety and depression that had been building up. Once again, I realized, my actions had hurt someone I cared for.

We reached the outskirts of Hue, and the rain let up a little as we wove our way into the city. The traffic was light on this early Sunday afternoon, and we were soon cruising along Tran Hung Dao Street beside the Song Huong River. This majestic waterway, which rolls grandly past lush green parks, serene temples, and riverside cafés, is popularly called the Perfume River, because flowers from upstream orchards fall into the water, creating a perfumed aroma. I was looking forward to a quiet afternoon that would allow me to ease back into the seclusion that had been interrupted by the social scene in Lang Co. We seemed to be nearing the downtown section of town when Ngo made an unexpected left turn and headed up a side street. We rode past a cluster of private homes until we came to a small two-story hotel on a residential street corner. The hotel manager in Lang Co had suggested this place, and I was glad it was in a quiet area.

A short sidewalk led from the street to the hotel entrance. Inside, I found a large, comfortably appointed sitting room with a few chairs and a small bar with three stools. Several brightly colored bottles of Vietnamese hooch were displayed above the bar. The reception desk was tucked into a small alcove, and a young woman sitting behind the desk greeted me. She was very friendly and made a point of saying she was glad to have an American guest so she could practice her English. The cost of a room was fifteen dollars a night, and although I knew I could have found cheaper accommodations, I was happy to have landed in tranquil surroundings. I gladly agreed to the rate, climbed the stairs, and was pleased to find my room tucked into a far corner of the rear corridor. The blue-walled space was small but clean, with a chair and a writing desk beneath a window looking out over neighboring homes. I took time unpacking my few belongings, then wrote a letter to Barbara. I wasn't sure if she'd receive it before I returned home in nine days, but I was feeling my love for her and Claire and needed to tell them so.

My mood was starting to sink, so I picked up one of my tour books and thumbed through to the section on Hue. My poor sleep of the night before must have caught up with me, though, because the next thing I knew, it was 5:00 in the evening and the book lay closed on my chest. My body felt grungy from not bathing in the last two days, but a long shower and a few stretches seemed to help. Soon I made my way to the lobby to see if anything was going on. Several folks were sitting there, all Vietnamese. One of the men had purchased a bottle of Nep Cam, a strong rice wine with a 30 percent alcohol content, and was offering drinks to everyone. After the night in Lang Co, I had little taste for alcohol, so I made do with a sip. Others refilled their glasses several times, and the atmosphere in the room became increasingly jovial over the next hour. The hotel had a contract with a nearby restaurant, so I was able to order some rice and chicken for dinner. By the time darkness fell, the sitting area had emptied. My mind was anything but empty, however, still churning with all I had experienced in the past few days. Not ready for bed, I decided to take a stroll before returning to my room.

The street was dimly lit and the sidewalk empty as I headed toward the Perfume River. When I arrived, I paused to listen to the faint watery murmur, contemplating the many centuries of life that had flowed across its silvery surface. In that moment, time seemed as vast as the night sky, and I rested for several minutes in its dark immensity, wondering what Hue would bring me in the coming days.

I was about halfway back to the hotel when a lone cyclist rode up behind me. The darkness prevented me from seeing the rider's face, but when the bike slowed, a female voice called out, "You want boom-boom? Two dollar. Very good." The abruptness of her appearance startled me, and I said nothing, which caused her to repeat the offer, "Boom-boom. You like. Two dollar." Declining the offer, I quickened my pace and was glad for the welcoming light at the hotel entrance.

CH 30
MARCH 14, 1996-*Hue, Vietnam*

Waking up the next day, I was glad to find sunny skies after the previous day's heavy rain. I was also glad to be in Hue, which was the last stop planned on my trip. Hue had been a point of interest for me years earlier because I already knew a bit about Vietnam's history and the central place Hue occupied in the country's formation. The area has been populated for several millennia, with China controlling large portions of what eventually became Vietnam from 111 BCE until 938 AD. As in Europe, various invasions and regional wars continuously shifted the borders and political identifications over the centuries. Hue had been declared the capital of a unified Vietnam from 1802 to 1945.

The French began their incursion into the country in the mid-nineteenth century, and mostly dominated the area until their defeat in the Battle of Dien Bien Phu in 1954. Following France's ouster, the United Nations Geneva Peace Accords split Vietnam into two nations: Hanoi became the northern capital, and Saigon was made the capital in the south. This arrangement was unacceptable to the northern government, which immediately initiated a guerrilla warfare campaign to reunite the country. And so began the Vietnam War (referred to as "the American War" by most Vietnamese).

The famous Imperial City was constructed between 1805 and 1832 to house the imperial family and serve as an administrative seat of power. The giant fortress known as the Citadel (measuring ten kilometers long and twenty kilometers wide) was constructed around the city. There are roughly three main sections of this massive complex: the first is the towering walls of the fortress itself (completed in 1833); the second is composed of various grandly constructed buildings where the civil and administrative work was carried out; and the third was the Purple Forbidden City, which housed the living quarters of the various emperors and their families.

As fascinating as all that was, what interested me most about Hue was what happened on January 31, 1968, when the Tet Offensive began. On that day several thousand NVA and Viet Cong soldiers under the leadership of the People's Army of Vietnam (PAVN) invaded the major cities of Vietnam, instigating a series of nationwide battles that continued for weeks. Hue was hit particularly hard, leaving the city, as one columnist put it, "a blown-out shell of smoldering rubble."

Prior to the Tet Offensive, fighting had been waged primarily in the countryside. That changed with Tet, and from then on the war broadened to include the entire country, rural and urban. The fighting was particularly fierce in Hue, where the battle went on for over a month. When the U.S. and South Vietnamese forces eventually retook Hue from the PAVN, eighty percent of the buildings had been either destroyed or badly damaged, and over five thousand civilians had died, including two thousand summarily executed by PAVN forces, whose own fatalities totaled anywhere from five to eight thousand (depending on the reporting source). U.S. and allied fatalities numbered 668, and the total number of wounded on all sides reached into the tens of thousands.

It was a horrific story, signaling the beginning of the end for the allied forces. The following year my battalion's mission was to intercept NVA soldiers retreating from the second Tet Offensive (these spring offensives continued until the war's end). The writing was on the wall, and on March 29, 1973, the U.S. finally withdrew its forces from Vietnam.

I was determined to carry out Johnny's request before exploring the city and visiting Tu Hieu, so I set off after a late breakfast, strolling along the impeccably swept Tran Hung Dao Street. Reaching the Ngo Mon Gate of the Citadel, I paid my three-dollar admission fee and entered the premises. The only word I can find to describe my initial impression is *grandeur*. The grounds of the Citadel measure over six miles in circumference, with lavishly spaced, sprawling lawns; colorful flower beds; monumental buildings; and gates, bridges, and moats connecting various sections of the property. The structures and massive archways were so beautifully designed that they reminded me of the largest churches I had seen in Italy, though the sheer magnitude of these grounds far surpassed anything I'd encountered in Europe. Stepping onto a neatly swept pathway, I continued on, noting there was still shell damage to some of the buildings from past fighting.

I could only imagine the imperial life that took place in such opulent structures in former times. But as majestic as this UNESCO landmark was, I couldn't muster any great interest in the imperial history these remarkable buildings represented. I'd come to abhor dynastic wars and the inevitable human subjugation resulting from them, and I was probably too American in my beliefs to be taken in by kingly realms. I knew why I was there, and it wasn't to moon over past glories, but to fulfill the request of my client who needed to return a piece of Vietnam that had been eating at him for twenty-eight years.

I wandered for a long while, strolling along winding walkways that eventually led to the rear of the compound where the property opened into pristine lawns and several well-spaced gardens. Approaching the far wall, I came to a newly tilled plot. The cultivated area was laid out in a couple dozen rows comprising a well-plowed rectangle with a perimeter of about ten by twenty meters. Looking around, I saw that no one was in sight and decided this would be the resting place for Johnny's keepsake.

I walked around the plot, knelt at the end, and slipped out of my backpack the little box Johnny had given me. The box was the size of a card deck, maybe a little wider, wrapped in black electrician's tape. Looking around again, I scooped into the loose earth with both hands, digging out a nice-sized hole until I reached hard ground. Using a pocketknife I'd purchased in Hoi An, I dug deeper, carving out a four-inch hole in the compacted earth. Scraping the sides clear, I looked around again and tore away the tape Johnny had used to seal his long-held memento.

The box nearly crumbled in my fingers, making me wonder how long it had been sealed, and whether Johnny had ever opened it since first taping it shut. His instructions were to open the box, then toss it away because only what was *in* the box mattered. He never said what that was, either in the group or in individual sessions, but his eyes always went a little blank when the subject of the box came up. He would acknowledge that he was holding something back, but would never name it.

I couldn't help wondering what it was that had so gripped him. My mind came up with all kinds of things: a flower, a photo, a piece of jewelry. The box wasn't big enough to have much in it, but its contents sure had Johnny hooked, and I noticed my hands trembling a bit as I held it. Opening the lid, I felt a small, irregularly shaped object covered with a scrap of old newspaper. The paper had Vietnamese writing on it, and I was pretty sure it was dated 1968 (the year of Johnny's tour). Interest piqued, I picked away the paper. What I found was something that had never even crossed my mind: a human bone.

It was a small bone, about three inches long, thinly curved and jagged at the end as if it were the winning half of a wishbone-pulling contest. I knew the fragment was human because the moment I saw it, I knew what it was and where it was from. Johnny had told me privately of a particularly gruesome experience he'd had in the war. He worked in highway construction and repair and had served in an area a few kilometers from Hue. It was hard, dangerous work, and the military used long-range artillery to beat back the continual harassment from enemy forces throughout the countryside. The Viet Cong were active in the neighboring hamlets, enhancing their opposition to the American invaders by whatever means necessary. Those who resisted the Cong's demands were subject to threats, violence, and often death.

The only part of the work Johnny liked was getting to meet the Vietnamese living close to where his unit worked. There was one village he particularly liked because he'd developed a relationship with one of the families. They had even invited him for dinner once, and Johnny swore it was the family dog they served, because their mongrel pet (named Dung) hadn't been around all evening.

A couple of months later, it became clear that Johnny's village was being used as a focal point of the Cong offensive. After negotiations with village elders, U.S. military personnel made it clear that they had no power to change the situation, so the Military Command decided to eliminate the village by firing in barrages of 155mm artillery rounds to take out every hootch in the little compound. The villagers—about a hundred farmers and their families—were given fair warning and allowed to leave with their personal belongings. Having no choice, they vacated the grounds and retreated to a grove of alder trees about fifty meters outside the village.

The time for the surgical strike came, and the people huddled within the grove, waiting for the earth-shattering eruptions, knowing that after the attack their lives would never be the same. What they did not know was that the artillery coordinate was off by a fraction. The missiles came precisely on time, but not on the specified target, and the thunderous rounds tore into the alder trees and the displaced peasants cowering within the grove.

Word of the atrocity immediately spread around the area, and Johnny's unit was paving a nearby road when they heard. His people were sent to clear the "debris," so he literally walked through a level of carnage more vast than anything he had experienced in combat. It was an area no larger than a schoolyard, he said. The trees were bent and gouged by shrapnel, but it was what was *on* the trees that became branded on his mind. Pieces of meat hanging from the lifeless branches, arms and legs still dripping with blood drenching the forest floor. There were a few recognizable bodies, but most of the carnage was bloody viscera splattered like coagulated paste over the butchered foliage.

Johnny had shared this in only the most general terms, but he had said nothing about bringing home a souvenir of the massacre. I now understood he had preserved a tiny relic of that fateful day to honor his lost friends and the horror that had obliterated their village. Holding the bone as reverently as I would a Communion wafer, I placed it gently at the bottom of the hole and covered it with the earth I'd removed, hoping it would stay buried when the bed was plowed again. Then I shoveled in the cultivated soil and rearranged it into its fluffy row. I felt I should say something then, find words to bless the lost lives represented by the tiny bone fragment. But no words came, just deep sadness for what had happened that day, and for the suffering caused by all the wars our deluded species continues to inflict upon itself.

I knelt there for a long time, watching my mind conjure up memories of other atrocities I knew about. These had been perpetrated by all sides of the conflict (as the young doctor at Peace Village had assured me), so there was no high ground for one side or the other. The My Lai massacre, in which five hundred Vietnamese civilians were killed by U.S. forces, was just the largest and most famous example. But there were so many more, including the massacre of two thousand civilians by the PAVN forces during Tet.

So many stories had come through my office in the years of my PTSD work, and as I knelt by that unplanted garden, those images started welling up in my awareness like toxic vomit. I remembered a vet relating how one of his comrades had gotten separated from his unit in a firefight and was captured by the NVA. When the U.S. forces finally rousted the enemy, they found their missing comrade impaled through his anus on a wooden stake, with the skin of his chest hanging in shreds. His captors had cut a deep horseshoe-shaped wound into his chest, then used pliers to peel the skin off his body. He didn't survive, but that image infected the memories of his buddies who had to pull him off the stake.

I remembered hearing Jon Cavaiani speak. He was a Medal of Honor recipient who for several years had been held in a Vietnamese prison camp sarcastically named the Hanoi Hilton. He said he couldn't speak of the torture his captors inflicted on him because there were children in the audience. He wept openly, and with great honor, as he related this.

I recalled two separate incidents when U.S. soldiers had used knives to slowly stab women to death in front of their children. Both were attempts to get information on the enemy's location. I don't know if their efforts were successful, but both soldiers are still plagued by the horrified faces of the children as they watched their mothers being so brutally murdered.

I thought of Norman, a tank commander during the battle for Hue. His armored unit rumbled down those beautiful streets fighting the PAVN forces who fired back with rocket-propelled grenades. Norman told how the enemy forces gathered children together, binding them with a rope around one wrist, then herding them onto sidewalks so they could use them for cover as they attacked the tanks from behind. They assumed that Americans would not fire into the group of children. This may have worked with some of the tankers, but it didn't work for Norman, who told us of how he had run his tank over the captured kids, crushing them to death to get at the enemy soldiers behind them. His eyes were always inflamed as he told this, his voice rising in a note of pleading, as if to ask, "What could I do?" He kept saying, "What could I do?"

No one had an answer.

I remembered Philip, the young Marine whose parents had both served in the Marine Corps, instilling such pride in the young man that he volunteered for Nam as an MP (Military Policeman).

Soon after arriving, he was ordered to help an ARVN lieutenant question some NVA prisoners. He expected to learn some effective interrogation techniques to extract information from POWs. Instead, what he witnessed was a long night watching electric wire being wound around the prisoners' genitals, long after they had coughed up whatever meagre "intelligence" they had. Philip did nothing to stop the torture and later reported the abuse to his commanding officer, who told him, "Welcome to Vietnam" and sent him on another assignment. That incident had cost Philip his pride in himself and in the Corps, and he had lived with the shame for decades. His alcoholism and three failed marriages reflected that loss of self-esteem.

I thought of the veteran who claimed he had captured a young Vietnamese woman and dragged her into an abandoned hootch, cutting off both of her breasts and raping her throughout the afternoon. He had come in one time, insisting on telling his story in graphic detail. After that session I never saw him again.

I remembered other rapes some of my vets reported, and I thought of Opey's recovered memory of the time he and two other Marines had carried a young woman into the brush to rape her. He recalled the scene vividly but had forgotten that a lieutenant had intervened to prevent the atrocity. For twenty-five years Opey, believing the rape had actually occurred, hated himself for it. Realizing it had not been physically completed did little to appease his conscience, because the act had already been carried out in his heart.

There had been too many acts of violence against civilians to count. Ron had turned eighteen a week before arriving in-country. He told of the many times he'd ridden in the back of a truck, hurling heavy cans of C-rations into the faces of hungry Vietnamese kids chasing the truck. To this day, he couldn't say why he'd done it, except that it was the way he'd been taught by the older grunts.

I thought of the Tay Ninh hillside where hundreds of peasants had been stranded in a defoliated area with an open latrine ditch. Many had been there for years, we were told.

I also remembered the last NVA prisoner I had treated a couple of weeks before getting wounded. The lead element of our column had spotted two NVA soldiers crossing a field of elephant grass and had opened fire. One was killed instantly, and the other went down with an abdominal wound and a shattered arm. Still holding his AK-47, he refused our commands to release it so we could tend to his wounds. As the company medic, I was called to the clearing to treat our prospective prisoner. When I got there, Captain Bates' voice was screaming through the company radio for us to take the prisoner alive. He actually said that any man killing "my gook" would be disciplined with an Article 15. Knowing that the battalion COs had an ongoing competition for who captured the most prisoners, we understood the reason for our Captain's concern very well.

Something snapped in me when I heard that. I was sick of being under the control of both our officers and the NVA, done with being told where to go and what to do. I decided to disarm the prisoner myself. So putting my M-16 on full auto (20-round output in 2.1 seconds), I stepped into the clearing and walked slowly toward the downed soldier, speaking softly, telling him in a language he couldn't understand to give up his weapon. My rifle was aimed straight at him, and if he had moved to fire, I would have lit him up like a Roman candle. Three steps, four steps, crooning to the young soldier, asking him to give it up so I didn't have to kill him. Our eyes were locked, and when I got within ten feet, he finally pushed his AK-47 away. I kicked it aside and called for our guys to come out and secure the area.

My treatment of that soldier was brusque and uncaring. So much had happened since my first encounter with wounded NVA soldiers that my attitude toward them had changed, especially after seeing so many of our own guys wounded or killed. I remember slapping on a couple of field dressings and moving his broken arm more roughly than necessary to get it splinted. In retrospect I felt terrible about that incident, because I had violated my standard of responsibility as a medic. It also opened my eyes, in a very personal way, to how easy it is to morally decompensate in a war situation.

I've thought often about that incident, and wondered what would have happened if I hadn't been wounded a short time later. Would I have become an abuser of the enemy casualties it was my job to treat? Thankfully, that's a question I never had to answer. Of all the people I met in Vietnam (excluding Michael MacParlane), it is this man to whom I am most indebted. His surrender to my unnecessary challenge saved his life and prevented me from committing a wanton act that would have haunted me for the rest of mine. Years later when I started the vet work, this insight became very helpful because many of my clients had issues about their treatment of the Vietnamese.

On and on, the memories gushed, spewing their flood of red horror. The veterans' stories felt like coagulated poison festering in my gut, but as I continued kneeling beside that unplanted garden, my mind gradually drifted from the distant past to my current life. Now that my mission for Johnny had been carried out, it was time to address my issues with Barbara and Claire. I had little idea of how to do this but hoped my experience at the Tu Hieu monastery might provide a clue on how to find healing for my family.

More than anything, I felt deep regret that I'd allowed the war's toxicity to follow me home and infect my loved ones. It had been such a long path from Military Avenue to the Sierra Nevada foothills, and something had obviously gotten twisted along the way. When Claire was born, I vowed to protect her from the world. As it turned out, I couldn't even protect her from myself.

CH 31
MARCH 14, 1996–*Hue, Vietnam*

Eventually I rose from the garden and walked quickly away, not looking back. Making my way toward the Citadel gate, I saw other tourists *oohing* and *aahing* about the magnificent structures. They were amazed at the architectural splendor, but all I could think of was the decrepit moral architecture of a humanity so addicted to war that it embraces mass murder as an acceptable means of resolving conflict.

I had no idea what I'd do for the rest of the day and was so lost in my despairing thoughts, I didn't even see the three young women who were coming toward me. They were girls, actually, probably in their late teens, and they stepped in front of me as we were about to pass. Groaning inwardly, I braced myself for another sexual come-on.

The girls were dressed casually in soft cotton shirts and modern form-fitting slacks, their hair either hanging loose or cut shorter around the ears. It took me a moment to realize one of them was addressing me. She was obviously the spokesperson for the group, tall and slender and more self-possessed than the other two, who hung back as their friend spoke for them. Looking me straight in the eye (unusual for young Vietnamese women), she announced in fractured English that they were students at the university and had been told to find an English-speaking foreigner who would help them practice their language skills. Would I be that person?

My first reaction was annoyance at being jolted out of my dark introspection, tempting me to pretend I was German and didn't know what she was saying. But they seemed so sincere in the way they presented their request that I couldn't resist their desire to learn and enhance their lives. My mind suddenly went to the Vietnamese women and children who had befriended me in the hospital, and what a gift that contact had been. It was clear I was being offered something beyond casual conversation and would be foolish to pass up the opportunity.

"I will talk with you on one condition," I said. "I help you with your English and you help me speak Vietnamese. Okay?" This seemed to surprise them, but they readily agreed and suggested we find a quiet area where we could sit and chat. And that's just what we did. Making our way to a small sitting area with a concrete bench and a couple of chairs, we sat in a rough circle and began our mutual lesson. We began by comparing names of simple things like *comb, pen,* and *book*, then talked about what life was like in our different countries. "Do all American teenagers really have cars when they turn sixteen?" they asked. Do they all use drugs? Do all Vietnamese kids live with their parents until they get married? We stopped repeatedly to explain words and phrases, and it was clear we all found this approach more interesting than simply naming objects. At one point, I mentioned figures of speech, giving an example of an American idiom and asking about theirs. Why say that someone "has a lot on the ball" when they are not playing a sport? And why do the Vietnamese say that someone is bad at rowing a boat but good at pushing it (i.e., bad at a job but good at making excuses)? We all started cracking up as example followed example, and, as is often the case with humor, the girls relaxed as we continued our discussion. I asked them if they had boyfriends, and this elicited shy laughter with the admonition that they were only beginning college and could only "look" until their studies were completed.

They asked me why I was in Hue, and I had to pause. I didn't want to shock them by mentioning I'd just buried a bone that was a relic from an atrocity perpetrated against their people. But their inquiry was legitimate and deserved an answer. Finally I just said I had come to the Citadel to pray for the people killed during the American War. This interested them because they wanted to know how Americans prayed. I told them I didn't really know how others prayed and actually didn't pray much myself, but I was interested in Buddhism. Did they know of Thich Nhat Hanh? Only one of the girls, the original spokesperson, said that she did, and asked about my experience studying Buddhism. I confessed I was not a Buddhist and had little understanding of the religion. She then surprised us all by suggesting we get on bikes and visit the temple attended by her family. I told her I had no bike, but she said it wasn't a problem, because I could use her bike and she would ride with one of the other girls.

We retrieved their bikes from an outdoor rack and off we went, pedaling about a mile down Tran Hung Dao Street to a small but lovely temple across from the Perfume River. The pagoda's simple verandah was exquisitely clean, and though the area was small, it felt spacious, with small, symmetrically spaced Bonsai trees, flowering plants, and a few benches. The meditation hall was open, and we walked into a large room with meditation mats stacked along the walls. A large statue of the Buddha surrounded by children graced the altar directly in front of us.

Two of the girls were hanging back, but the one whose temple it was sank to her knees, prostrating herself before the statue. Rising, she looked at me. I froze in momentary indecision. My belief in Christianity had waned over the years, but paying homage to a foreign god marked a turning point I wasn't sure I was ready to cross (later I learned that the Buddha isn't considered a god, simply a devoted human who found the way through delusion to inner peace). Engaging in a strange religious practice felt disloyal, and I balked at going further. In my hesitation, I remembered a story told by Rachel Naomi Remen, an American physician who works with people suffering from terminal illness. One of her Jewish patients asked his rabbi about the propriety of worshipping with members of other faiths. "Strangers," he called them. "Philip," the rabbi had answered, taking the man gently by the shoulders, "God does not make strangers, *you* make strangers."

So I surrendered my resistance, sinking to my knees, then lowering my entire body to the floor. After the emotional turmoil at the Citadel, I was tight as a coiled spring, but as I eased onto the tiles, my belly seemed to relax a bit. Breathing into the feeling, I sensed the relaxation spreading and remained prostrated for several breaths, enjoying a momentary respite from the adrenalin still firing in my nervous system.

When I finally rose, the girls were looking at me with concern. It was obviously unusual to remain prostrated for that long, and they didn't seem to know what to make of my prolonged bow. I didn't either, so I just smiled and motioned for us to go outside. We sat on the veranda, mostly quiet among the flowering plants, serenaded by the chirping of birds in nearby trees. Taking time to appreciate such simple pleasures was not the norm in my high-pressured life, and I found it uncomfortable to relax silently with others. But as with my earlier hesitation, the feeling soon eased, and I was able to settle into quiet time with my young friends. They certainly had no problem surrendering to the moment, and seeing the radiant serenity in their faces helped me relax into peace.

No monk or other official appeared, so we stayed until one of the girls, looking at her watch, spoke to her friends. Climbing back on our bikes, we began our ride back to the Citadel. It was already 1:30 when we got there, and the girls announced that they needed to go home for the lunch their mothers had prepared. Yes, they said, each of them still lived at home and would continue doing so for as long as they remained at the university. I was sad to say good-bye but wished them the very best in their lives and studies.

I spent the rest of the afternoon hiking around the downtown area, not seeking attractions or historical landmarks, just watching the busy folks and perusing the shops. I remember being struck by how similar that scene was to the typical rush of American cities. The crowds may have been larger here, but all in all it was just people moving about their community, engaged in the simple commerce of being alive. Wandering away from downtown, I strolled along the Perfume River, thinking about the unexpected relaxation I'd experienced at the temple. I wasn't sure how that had happened or what it meant, but I was grateful for the encounter with the girls after getting slammed by the war memories after burying Johnny's bone. The sense of peace that had come over me while I was prostrating was a different matter, and I truly didn't know what to make of that. The feeling seemed to come from nowhere, and I had no idea why it had happened or how to get it back.

I stayed in that night, sitting at the hotel bar making small talk with a few other guests, including the Chinese guy who told me he was driving his car to Ho Chi Minh City soon. He invited me to ride with him, but I said I had matters to complete in Hue and wasn't sure how long that would take. He had plenty of time, he said, and could wait for a few days before leaving. That surprised me, and I wondered if he had an ulterior motive. He told me that he'd traveled to other Southeast Asian countries for business but had never been to America, and he was very interested in how people lived there. I had the sense that he was seeking a business opportunity, hoping I might assist him in some way. At this point in my life, I was having trouble assisting myself, so I told him that I had other plans. The conversation drifted to other topics, and he eventually excused himself, saying that he had an appointment the next morning and needed his sleep. I spent a few minutes chatting to the hotel clerk, the same friendly young woman I'd met the previous day. She, too, seemed glad for the chance to practice her English.

A few minutes after 9:00 I decided to take a walk before turning in. I went down the street a couple of blocks, thinking about my visit to the Tu Hieu monastery the next day. Thich Nhat Hanh had been exiled by the communist government for several years, so he wouldn't be present. He had since founded a monastery in France that attracted seekers from around the world. I wasn't sure what

I'd find at Tu Hieu, but I had the strongest intuition that Tu Hieu was a place I needed to experience.

I was approaching the hotel entrance when a bicycle passed, then stopped in front of me. A familiar voice called out, "Hey you, boom-boom, two dollar. Very nice, you like." She turned the front wheel in toward me, blocking the sidewalk, as Oy had done at the Hoi An barbershop. The hotel lighting illuminated her face, and I could see that she was middle-aged, short and stout, with a wrinkled face and eyes that were utterly impassive. Leaning forward on the handlebars, she repeated her offer. Her voice was so dispassionate, I had the sense that she could have been selling anything from costume jewelry to pickled squid. I felt a wave of compassion because here she was, peddling herself from a bicycle, and I told her I was married, showing her my wedding ring, and was not interested in sex. Speaking softly, I expressed how sorry I was for her plight, nearly crooning as I told her that she was a good person and I wished her well.

Her eyes dropped as I spoke, the brow wrinkling as if concentrating on my words. I had the sense that she was affected by my words and might reply in a meaningful way. Finally her eyes rose and she looked me straight in the eye, asking flatly, "Young boy? You want young boy? Young girl? Very easy, I get."

A long moment of silence pervaded the space between us. Having nothing more to say, I could only shake my head and go inside.

CH 32
MARCH 15, 1996–*Hue, Vietnam*

The next day I was pretty wasted but, after groaning my way out of the brain fog, decided to visit Tu Hieu Monastery that afternoon. Mainly I was emotionally depleted by my experience at the Citadel and was struck by the fact that every stage of my journey seemed to bring a confusing mixture of hope and despair. This new Vietnam was vastly more complicated than what I'd imagined, and I wondered if what I'd find at the monastery would provide any clarity about the country or about my life. Just thinking of this made me nervous because I had only a few days before my flight back to California, and I was aware that nothing I'd experienced so far was providing insight on how to heal my family wounds.

The hotel had bread, lettuce rolls, and other finger food, so I ate quietly, sipping my coffee and looking at the tour book to see what I might do. There were tons of suggestions, but I wasn't in a sightseeing mood, preoccupied as I was with the day ahead. After breakfast I started walking and decided to let the morning take care of itself. The weather was still clear, making the seven-block walk downtown an easy stroll. The streets got busier as the houses thinned out, replaced by several cafés and a variety of stores and offices. I was burned out from all the visual input I'd absorbed in the last two weeks, and I couldn't muster up any interest in my surroundings. I spent a couple of hours ambling through the streets, not seeking attractions or historical landmarks, just watching the people going about their business. Along the way I chatted with a couple of younger Vietnamese who spoke limited English and wanted to interact with the lone foreigner in his strange Free Tibet cap. The language barrier didn't allow for any in-depth discussion, but I enjoyed the amiable contacts. The two young men both seemed to believe that China had no business invading Tibet, and I wondered if the Western invasion of their country influenced their opinion.

At one point, I stopped for a snack at the Lac Thien restaurant, which was run by a family of deaf mutes. The place was renowned in the tour books for having the best banana pancakes on earth and donuts beyond compare. Both turned out to be true. My taste buds rose to the occasion, and I was in hog heaven, wiping syrup off my plate and watching two of the brothers operating the open kitchen. Both wore aprons over brightly colored t-shirts and white chef hats. Working seamlessly in the tiny space, they seemed more a single unit than a duo as they danced around each other to serve up their tasty dishes.

Pushing back my plate, I noticed a young Caucasian at the next table and struck up a conversation. He looked a bit wilted—a thin guy with slumped shoulders, gazing at me through rheumy, blood-shot eyes. Jason was twenty-five, he told me, and had been traveling alone through China for six weeks. He explained that he'd sched-uled his trip after getting jilted by his fiancée, who had dumped him for his best friend. It was a major blow, and he had attempted suicide by taking an assortment of pills that put him down but not out. After he woke up in the emergency room, he was put on a 72-hour hold and told to see a psychiatrist when he was released.

He soon felt himself sinking again and knew something had to change. The medical personnel had been kind, but Jason wasn't having any of it. He didn't want meds and didn't want therapy. All he wanted was to get out of Des Moines, Iowa, and lose himself in a new environment. He'd always been interested in China and thought that Asia might be large enough to contain his grief. The journey had been going well, but then he'd come down with a seri-ous intestinal infection that quickly intensified. He was so sick that he couldn't even make it to the next stop on the hiking trail. He'd had to sleep outside, shivering and scared for his life.

The next day he staggered into a little farm village, cramped in pain and bleeding out of his ass. Two old sisters who lived alone took the trembling white boy in, feeding him herbal remedies when he was delirious and drenched in sweat. He was barely conscious for days, he said, thrashing and moaning in agony. Eventually his fever broke and he was able to ingest some of the rich soups the old women offered. He started feeling better, and as he recovered, he remembered that in the depth of the delirium he had had an insight that would change his life.

"I was about gone," Jason said, "completely out of my body. Didn't even know where I was. Part of me wanted to just give it up and let the infection take me, and I damn near did. But I kept coming up against something I can't even describe—something that wouldn't let me go."

He was speaking slowly, his eyes on mine, but also seemed to be looking out somewhere beyond the room. "In the end I realized I wasn't just the victim of a fucked-up story. It was my choice whether I lived or died." Jason was silent for several moments before continuing. "Everybody has to surrender sometime," he said, raising his eyes. "I remember the exact moment the fever broke and something deep inside shifted. Basically, I surrendered to life."

After a few more days recovering, Jason knew he had to face the life he had been trying to escape. He was going home to apply for grad school, he said, and chart a new course for the future. After finishing his story, he was done with the conversation and left to catch a flight to Ho Chi Minh City. It was an amazing tale, and I found it surprising that he could share such intimate details with a stranger. But then I saw it was a story that needed to be told, and a stranger in a strange land was likely the perfect person to share such a deep experience with. The word *surrender* triggered my memory of the experience I'd had prostrating at the temple, making me wonder about my own situation.

But not wanting to get caught up in more sad reflections, I left the café and started walking to my hotel. On the way back, I stopped at a street vendor's makeshift kitchen and ate two bowls of thick soup to balance all the sugar and chocolate I'd consumed.

It was two o'clock when I returned to my room, and I rested on the rumpled twin bed, so swamped in thought that I couldn't even register what my mind was saying. Jason's story of how it took a life-threatening illness to make him see that *he* had the choice to live or die had sent shivers down my spine. For years I'd been running on adrenalin and endurance, obsessing on a mission that was deadening my heart and damaging my family. His tale made me realize I also had choice, and that I could not deny my plight as the life-and-death struggle it was. That seemed clear. The part that wasn't clear was what to do about it.

That question still boggled my mind, and it was a relief to know I didn't have to deal with it right at that moment. All I needed to do was get to Tu Hieu Monastery, and *that* was under my control. Since there was no point in waiting longer, I rose to begin the final leg of the journey, grabbing my water bottle and notebook as I headed for the door. I had scoped out where the monastery was—a few miles from the hotel, just beyond Hue's city limit. Stopping at the hotel's front desk, I arranged to borrow one of the bicycles they kept for guests. Most of the bikes in the rack looked rusty and somewhat dilapidated, but I found one with decent tires that seemed serviceable. Walking it into the street, I climbed on and started pedaling, noting how good it felt to be traveling under my own power after getting carted around on so many motorcycles. The route was very simple: back up Tran Hung Dao Street, a few lefts and rights through the dwindling neighborhoods, then a short ride past a few scattered homes and rice paddies into the countryside. The road soon narrowed into a two-way country lane meandering through light forest and a couple of high-grass meadows.

It didn't take long to come to the sign for the monastery. It was printed in Vietnamese, but the name "Tu Hieu" stood out. I'd read that the phrase literally means "piety through compassion," and that Thich Nhat Hanh represented the Mahayana school of Buddhism, which focuses on bringing loving kindness in action and thought into the world. Turning right, I glided into a large parking area where I found a couple of cars and a large bus with a placard above the windshield with lettering I recognized as German. Parking the bike next to the cars, I paused and scanned the lot. It was immaculately tidy and level all the way to the tree line.

I got off the bike and made my way to an arched gateway leading up a short flight of stairs to a building. There was no one in view, but I heard chanting from above and decided to check it out. At the top of the stairs, I came to the doorway of a closed room and paused. Since there was no one around to ask, I inched open the door and peered inside. The room was dark, so I stepped into a wide foyer for a better look, finding a room full of brown-robed monks sitting on meditation cushions. Their chanting was completely atonal—just a few dozen voices reciting verses in a language I later learned was Sanskrit. The entire room was dancing in flickering, candlelit shadows, with wisps of incense permeating the air. The monks were lined up in tidy rows, sitting on cushions placed on top of bamboo mats. My first impression was amazement at encountering a scene I had read about but never experienced.

Then I had a second reaction: revulsion.

As my eyes adjusted to the dim lighting, I saw several of the German tourists walking among the monks, bending and stooping with their cameras clicking away at the sedate faces. The contrast between the solemn monks and the crass tourists was startling. I recoiled as they zeroed in on the altar, statues, and beautiful wall hangings (thangkas), nearly stumbling over the narrow mats as they recorded images to share back home. It was a bizarre spectacle, and I felt a stab of disgust at the impertinent photographers.

Other than the tourists and the monks, the only person in the room was a woman standing a few feet away. She was dressed in a uniform that marked her as the group's bus driver. Astonished by what I was seeing, I barged into her personal space and pointed at the boorish tourists still invading the rows of monks.

"What are they doing?" I asked.

She regarded me impassively. Clearly misunderstanding my question, she gestured not toward the tourists but toward the seemingly unperturbed monks, who weren't missing a beat of their monotonal chant. Her voice was heavily accented when she answered, devoid of the slightest inflection, as if stating a simple fact that should have been obvious.

"They are praying for you," she said.

I was startled speechless by the unexpected reply. A long moment of silence passed between us, her eyes softening as if she were curious to know how I'd respond. But I had no response. Turning my head, I peered closer at the monks, so sedate as they recited their earnest prayer. The words flowed effortlessly, so blended I couldn't make out individual voices in the collective hum. Their postures were strong and straight, but also relaxed, as if perfectly balanced in their cross-legged sitting position. I was amazed at how attuned to their chanting they remained, seeming to not even notice the invasive tourists.

There was a sudden tap at my elbow, and I saw that one of the older monks had risen from his cushion and approached me from behind. He was tall and thin behind crooked wire-rimmed eyeglasses, probably a couple of decades older than my fifty years, and very gracious in his manner. Laying his right hand softly on my arm, he motioned with his left toward an empty cushion at the edge of a row, indicating that I was welcome to sit with the monks, who were finishing their chant and dropping into silent meditation. A golden bell was struck with a mallet, its reverberation sending waves of tranquility throughout the room. Confused by the monk's contact, I hesitated as he again gestured toward the empty mat. By this time the Germans had retreated to the end of the hall and were starting to file out the door. The silence following the chiming of the bell filled the room with a palpable stillness. Remembering my experience prostrating the day before, I accepted the monk's invitation and sat on the cushion. I had no idea what to do next. Bending over, the old monk looked me straight in the face as he took in an exaggerated breath, then released it with a slight whooshing sound. He did this three or four times, raising his right palm on the inhalation and lowering it with the exhalation.

"Just sit and breathe," I understood him to say. "Just sit and breathe." He watched me for a few moments, then indicated I was tensing my jaw by pantomiming rigidly clenched teeth on his own face. Feeling the tension, I relaxed the muscles around my mouth, which seemed to deepen my breathing. Satisfied, he returned to his own cushion a few feet away.

I had read that the goal of Buddhist meditation is to channel one's attention from thought to simple awareness, using the breath as the object of concentration. I had imagined the actual method would be much more complex, but I went with the program, focusing on the sensations of breathing—the slight tickle in my nose with the in breath, the coolness of my lips as the breath was released, the rising and falling in my belly and chest. I continued watching my breath for several minutes, feeling a gradual sense of relaxation that was probably more related to the monks' support than to my own effort. There was something about being included in that circle of devotees that created a sense of safety and belonging I hadn't known for a long time. Surrendering into that warmth, I was flooded by a relief so deep that it brought tears to my eyes. Every breath took me deeper as the meditation continued, opening me more and more fully to the silent companionship being offered by the monks.

The golden bell sounded again, and the meditation ended. The monks rose as one and started filing out a back door. Blinking into the candlelit dimness, I felt a wave of sadness at their departure, as if I were losing a trusted ally I'd just come to know. When the back door closed, I was alone in the room, absorbed in a silence so deep it seemed to permeate my entire body. For the first time in memory I was aware of having no thoughts bouncing around my mind, only a sense of wonder at what I'd just experienced.

Looking around, I noticed a young monk standing at the front door. He was about thirty, short, with a slight build and shaved head. He seemed to be waiting for me, but it wasn't clear whether he was sent to escort me off the property or engage in conversation. Either way, I was glad to finally have a personal encounter. Clumsily, I rose from the cushion, knees and ankles cracking as they readjusted from the unfamiliar sitting position. The monk motioned me outside, and we paused on the stair landing, he in his loose brown robe, me in my khaki shirt and Free Tibet cap. His English was quite limited, but he was very friendly, and I understood that he was welcoming me to the monastery.

He told me his name was Duc and asked how I had heard of Tu Hieu. When I told him I'd read about Thich Nhat Hanh and was interested in his teaching, Duc's eyes brightened. He asked if I was a student of Buddhism, and I said no, just an old vet interested in learning how Buddhism dealt with war and its aftermath. He nodded effusively and told me I was welcome to visit the monastery as often as I wished while in Hue. Our encounter was warm but hampered by our language difficulty, so our conversation quickly wound down. We said our farewell *tam biets*, and I told him I'd be back the following day.

Riding back from Tu Hieu, I felt the fresh, clean breeze against my face, and the pedaling so easy that it felt as if the bike were driving itself. I stopped once to sit next to an expansive rice paddy and contemplate what I'd just experienced at the monastery. There weren't a lot of thoughts churning in my mind, just a parade of rich sensory images: the candlelit room, wafts of pungent incense, the atonal chanting of the monks. It all felt somewhat magical and as though I'd been there for days, though I knew it had been barely more than an hour. At the same time, paradoxically, the calm stillness of the meditation hall contrasted with my excitement at being invited to return and continue sitting with the monks.

Soon I was rolling into the outskirts of town. It was nearly seven o'clock and I hadn't eaten since chugging down the soup after my sugar fest at the bakery, so I stopped at the first restaurant I came to. Following dinner, I pedaled slowly to the hotel, parked my bike in its rack, and took a short walk before going to my room. Eagerly anticipating the next phase of my journey, I turned in early and slept through the night.

CH 33
MARCH 16-19, 1996-*Tu Hieu Monastery, Vietnam*

I did return the next day, and for several thereafter.

Duc had told me there was a noon service, so I arrived late morning the next day and sat down on the same cushion I had used the day before. For a moment I was alone in the flickering candlelit shadows, then a rear door opened and in came the monks, swishing along in their loose brown robes, shaved heads inclined slightly forward. Transfixed by their slow procession around the altar, I noted how they were separate but seemed to move as one, more like the sinuous vertebrae of a single organism than like a line of individual monks.

The bell rang and the room filled with the slow, atonal cadence of their chanting. The unintelligible words were vaguely hypnotic but had little effect on me, making me impatient for the meditative stillness I'd experienced the previous day. When a second bell signaled the start of meditation, I was more than ready. Stiffening my spine, I willed myself to focus on my breath and drop into another round of inner peace.

Didn't happen.

On my first inhalation, thoughts started bouncing around in my head like pellets in a pinball machine. The objective may have been to dive into meditative bliss, but the mind refused to cooperate. It was that quick. Before I could exhale, I was swept up in a whirlwind of memories, plans, stories, family issues, images from the journey, the discomfort in my knees, what I was having for lunch, etc., etc. The list seemed endless, with no particular theme, just a relentless parade of incessant mind chatter, making it impossible to relax, let alone deepen.

Staying with the initial instruction, I continued to sit and breathe, but was constantly bombarded by one unwanted thought after another. It went on like that throughout the session: I'd take a breath, immediately become flooded with thought, recognize the distraction, and try to refocus. Over and over and over. Each time I'd bear down harder, only to get ambushed again by intrusive mind chatter. At one point I actually shook my head to dislodge the unwanted thoughts, but that didn't help either. I was extremely disappointed and couldn't understand what was happening. It was the same dimly lit room, the same monks, and the same incense, but my experience couldn't have been more different.

During the late afternoon sit my mind seemed quieter. Even so, intrusive thoughts kept popping up despite my effort to focus on the breath. On my first visit to the monastery, I'd obviously tapped into a vein of beginner's luck, and getting that initial taste of inner peace had motivated me to continue practicing the simple act of sitting and breathing. But that experience of inner peace hadn't lasted. Later I learned that confronting the chattering mind is exactly what meditation practice entails. The process can be frustrating, let alone humbling, because it shows how addicted the mind is to its incessant mental activity. It also reveals how averse most of us are to simply sitting in stillness.

Tending to the busy mind turned out to be my experience in all my subsequent meditations. It soon became clear that willing myself not to think wasn't helpful, but that it actually accelerated mental agitation. I also noticed that when I was tuned in to my breathing, not trying for any effect, fleeting moments of stillness seemed to come by surprise. They weren't dramatic, but a sweet clarity would open in my mind, free of the nagging thoughts that had plagued it a moment before. Then more thoughts, more effort, more frustration trying to maintain a focused mind.

It wasn't lost on me that this softer way of relating to myself was the complete opposite of how I'd been living for several years. The vet work had turned my life into a daily grind, and it was only through endurance and force of will that I had been able to maintain my unhealthy pace. Not struggling, even while meditating, actually felt foreign and contrived, though it was clear that's what was needed. The whole thing was mind boggling. The biggest obstacle to being still, I realized, was trying to make it happen.

Regardless of the difficulty, I was determined to explore this new way and see where it took me. The meditation sessions became the central focus of my stay at Tu Hieu, but it was during the time between services that I began sorting out the issues plaguing my life. For the first time in the journey, I settled into a predictable routine that was a relief after so much running around during the prior two weeks. After breakfast I'd either wander through neighborhoods of small single-story homes or amble along the banks of the Perfume River until I found a place to sit and write in my journal. The river, I found, was a perfect place to reflect on what I was experiencing at Tu Hieu.

After my morning walk, I'd bike to the monastery and take my seat on the mat, then tune into the chanting. I never did understand the words, but I tried to relax into the monotonal flow, letting its steady drone calm my mind in preparation for the silent sitting. The monks also did walking meditation. This seemed strange at first, but I came to enjoy walking around the zendo in single file, taking slow, mindful steps that seemed to epitomize the goal of staying in the present moment.

I was welcome to participate in the services, but in the time between I was totally on my own. The monks had their own lives and seemed to spend most of their time in other parts of the building. In his stumbling English, Duc informed me that they attended classes, engaged in other rituals, and performed chores in their highly regimented schedule.

Tu Hieu didn't provide lunch, so I needed either to pedal back to town or bring food with me. I quickly chose the latter in order to maintain the quiet solitude I was starting to appreciate. After years of heavy stress doing my vet work, quietness and solitude were unknown experiences, and I found myself increasingly drawn to the serene aura of the monastery.

As far as I could tell, there were few rules for guests, the assumption being that anyone willing to visit the monastery would honor its customs (the photo-snapping Germans were the only exception I witnessed). It had been made clear that I was free to wander the grounds and rest in the zendo, but should refrain from entering the cloistered areas. I violated this injunction just once, when the monks were taking their afternoon naps. Their communal bedroom had large open windows, and I walked by once, noting how motionless the twenty or so brown-robed monks were, lying side by side in the darkened room. Remembering the squirmy tykes in the Da Nang school, I couldn't help smiling at the monks' relaxed uniformity. Every aspect of their lifestyle seemed to enforce conformity to the group, seemingly to discourage individual identity in favor of the communal.

Since Duc's English was so limited and no one else spoke any English at all, there was virtually nobody to converse with. This was disconcerting at first but proved invaluable for the opportunity it provided for self-reflection. I soon fell into a rhythm of gathering with the monks for the meditations, then relaxing in the unstructured private time in the interval between services. I spent hours alone on the grounds, taking walks, reading, or just watching clouds and wondering at the passage of time. There were only five days before I'd be heading back to Ho Chi Minh City, and I wanted to get as much out of the experience as possible.

On my third day I found a book on my cushion titled *Being Peace*, written by Thich Nhat Hanh. Duc had left it for me, telling me later that it had been left by a previous visitor, and that I was free to read it while visiting the monastery. I was grateful for the opportunity to learn more about Buddhism. My intention was to read the book from cover to cover, but it quickly became clear that I was far too engrossed in my inner process to absorb that much cognitive input. Perusing it, two things stood out that altered the way I was viewing my situation.

The primary message was that in order to bring peace into our world and into our personal relationships, we first need to have peace within ourselves. His words reminded me of the airplane injunction that in an emergency we should put the oxygen mask on our own face before trying to help others. Whether it's oxygen or peace, we can only give what we already have.

That made sense to me because when I looked back on it, the last seven years had been anything *but* peace. I'd had a partner at first, but she had retired after a year, leaving me with her caseload on top of my own. I dug in doing the best I could and was soon seeing up to six traumatized vets a day, five days a week. A few of the guys were overtly suicidal, many were dealing with severe family crises, some had legal issues that needed resolving before other areas of their lives could be addressed. A few were homeless and had been living on the fringes of society for many years. The numbers were staggering, and my PTSD issues quickly escalated into an ongoing pattern of hypervigilance, monster mood swings, anger reactions, obsessive combat ideation, and nightly sleep disturbances that reawakened old nightmares (which often included scenes vets had related to me during the past week). It went on that way for years. At one point I hired a subcontractor, and when her caseload filled, I hired another. And the vets kept coming.

Before I knew it, I'd gone from being an attentive, loving father to a snarling recluse chasing ghosts around the house. At home or at work I was so wired that I overreacted to even the slightest disturbance to my rigid routine, including the normal childish behavior of my young daughter. The premise of Thich Nhat Hanh's book could not have been more right-on, and I had no peace to give.

The second thing that stood out from the book was the assertion that we need community to progress on our life paths, especially when things get difficult. Thich Nhat Hanh made the astute observation that we have to do our spiritual work by ourselves, but we can't do it alone. The bottom line is, everyone needs support. That hit me like a sledgehammer because it made me realize that I'd been going it totally alone doing the vet work. After my partner left, I bore down harder, trying to give the vets the best I had. As the pressures mounted up, however, and as I was increasingly overwhelmed by the intensity of each week, I started using alcohol to "relax" on the weekends. But the booze tended to exacerbate my eruptive behavior, and I often skipped engagements Barbara had planned, or I relied more heavily on alcohol to get through social gatherings I could barely tolerate. In this way I sank deeper and deeper into the chaotic inferno my life had become.

My behavior had gone out of control, and I badly needed help— healthy input from others who would challenge me to reevaluate the decisions I was making. What I had given myself instead was alternating bouts of mind-numbing isolation and emotional turmoil, pushing away even those I loved most. In my ruminations at Tu Hieu, I remembered my trip to the village barber in Hoi An. The despair I'd felt that morning had driven me out of myself to seek contact in the community. Doing so had eased my sense of alienation, making me see that willingness to take such risks was absolutely necessary if I wanted to reverse the downward spiral plaguing my life and family.

None of this was the fault of the vets, of course. Those men (and a very few women) were remarkably courageous in confronting both the past and the present, and it was a huge honor to be part of their recovery. The problem was, I wasn't seeing them as the wounded middle-aged adults they were, trying to get their lives in order. To me, they were the mangled grunts I hadn't been able to save in Vietnam.

In retrospect, I'm amazed that even with all the training I'd had, I couldn't see that it was my combat issues that were driving my disruptive behavior. But that's how PTSD works. When a traumatized person's existence is threatened, all emotions not connected to survival diminish to the point of insignificance. For years on end, although we weren't in a physically life-threatening situation, my nervous system was being triggered by the vets' stories as if we were facing annihilation from enemy fire.

All this was starting to become clear as I paused near the end of my journey. Tu Hieu had turned out to be a refuge I hadn't counted on, and the space it provided gave me the opportunity to reexamine my life and see the consequences of my compulsive behavior. *Being Peace* confronted me with the one insight I could no longer escape: in order to tend to the wounds of my family, I had first to tend to my own. And to do this, I needed to open myself to support from others.

In that vein, I couldn't help thinking about the conversation with Jason before my first visit to Tu Hieu. His story ended with his choosing life and making plans to reenter the world. As different as his situation was from mine, his story inspired me, and I wondered what that might mean for me.

My thoughts increasingly turned to my trip home and reconnecting with Barbara and Claire. I hadn't a clue how that was going to go, and although meditation seemed like a good start, I had no illusion that it was a silver bullet. Developing a sitting practice was definitely something I wanted to continue, but any true change would have to come in the working out of our ongoing relationships.

Although Tu Hieu was the center of my time in Hue, the evenings were open and I used the opportunity to explore more of the city's sights. On one occasion I joined a group taking a nighttime cruise on the Perfume River. We were a small, convivial group, but our chatting quieted down as the fifteen-foot boat reached midstream, leaving behind the city's bustling traffic. We were sailing under a waning moon that highlighted the shore lights, while gentle waves lapped against the hull, lulling me into a quiet reverie that felt as close to peace as anything I could remember. The anxiety I had been feeling about returning home seemed to melt away. Peering into the darkness, I was amazed that this unexpected serenity had come upon me so effortlessly. "Home," I began to see, was more a state of mind than a physical location.

On another evening I made my way to the dock area where houseboats were moored several meters offshore. A small crowd was milling about the area, and I happened to meet a young boy who asked if I was an American. Using his smattering of English, Ai told me his parents owned one of the houseboats and offered to take me in his rowboat to meet them. That sounded interesting, so we were soon paddling toward the vessels, which were higher than the ones I had seen in California, several with people sitting on the flat tops. Ai tied his rowboat next to a ladder, and we climbed up to meet his parents. They were extremely friendly but spoke no English. Given my relative seclusion at Tu Hieu, this presented no problem, so I settled in beside them, and we spent a half hour or so sitting quietly in the cool night air. A gentle breeze caressed us in the soft moonlight, accentuating the silence surrounding us. Smiling at Ai, I was grateful that he had introduced me to one more aspect of Vietnamese life.

When we were back in his rowboat, I told Ai that I'd like to take the oars, and he promptly complied by moving to the forward seat. The oars were set up to be used in a standing position, and it took a minute to get the hang of it, but I quickly got the boat headed toward the dock. Unfortunately, Ai darted past me to change positions, and I bopped him on the forehead, raising a small goose egg. I felt horrible about that, but he made nothing of it. Even so, I gave him two American dollars after we landed, and he seemed thrilled for the payment, immediately running off to show his friends.

On my last night in Hue, I decided to treat myself to a dinner at an upscale restaurant on the shore of the Perfume River. I'd been eating cheaply, and a bit of splurging seemed fitting to top off my sojourn in Hue. Perusing the menu the night before, I'd seen that a full course dinner could be had for around twelve dollars. I went early to avoid the crowds, walking under a well-lit entrance into the main dining room. Several tables, covered in fine linens and gleaming silver place settings, were already filled with diners, both Caucasian and Vietnamese. The noise level was disappointing, but I noticed a veranda overlooking the river and asked the gray-haired maître d' for a table there. He sat me at a railing overlooking the water, which was exactly what I wanted.

When he asked if I wanted a drink before dinner, I paused. Except for the scotch in Lang Co, I had been limiting myself to one beer or glass of wine a night, and I had pretty much abstained after arriving at Tu Hieu. I didn't feel there was anything wrong with knocking back a drink, but I also felt no need for alcohol, so I declined the offer.

The sun was just starting to set, casting glimmering ribbons of light across the waves that sloshed beneath my feet. The current was barely perceptible as it flowed toward the sea, five miles downstream. No one else was on the veranda. The setting could not have been more peaceful, but I couldn't relax my anxiety about returning home. The journey had affected me in ways I could feel but not explain, and my hope was that our family could begin an ongoing healing process that would carry us forward. But I was returning to the same situation I'd left three weeks ago, and I had no idea how things would go.

I thought about what I'd learned at Tu Hieu, and how that could guide me as I re-entered my life. I'd come to Vietnam asking for a solution to my problems, but that was not what I'd been given. Instead, I had received a direction, a clear sense that any true change would have to come from inside, and that my troubles were less about what the situation was than about how I was dealing with it. That made sense, but I wasn't all that clear on what it specifically meant in terms of my return home. Sighing into the fading light, I surrendered to the fact that there was a whole lot more I wasn't clear about and, feeling at a complete loss, I found myself yearning for a sign.

Yearning was a word I didn't remember ever having used before. Certainly I had wanted, desired, even craved things or outcomes I thought necessary for my happiness. But there was a difference here. What I was feeling at that moment went beyond the personal. Whatever yearning was, it opened my heart beyond the suffering of my small family to include razed Vietnamese villages, child prostitutes, global hunger, abused women, and dead babies. It included all the victims in our world and also the perpetrators (I later learned that Thich Nhat Hanh had written about this in a poem titled "Call Me by My True Name").

So much suffering, nothing excluded. The experience was effortless but profound. I simply yearned for the suffering to end.

Shifting in the chair, I gazed out over the gentle waves and felt my belly loosen. Gradually the worrisome thoughts seemed to evaporate, and a sense of clarity settled into the space where those thoughts had been. Continuing to compulsively plow through my intense therapy schedule was a recipe for chaos and reactivity. The direction offered by Tu Hieu actually seemed quite simple. The softening needed to relax into meditation was exactly the quality I needed to incorporate into my home and work life. And as I had realized earlier, to do this this I needed to surrender my isolation and find support from the community.

After the noon sit tomorrow, I'd board a train for Da Nang, where I'd spend the night before flying back to Ho Chi Minh City. My journey was ending, and I hadn't even begun understanding how it had affected me. There was no doubt it was going to take a long time to integrate all I'd been through. But it was all more than I could think about, so, mercifully, I didn't. A party of four was being seated across from me on the veranda, and it was a pleasure to hear their murmuring voices as I surrendered to the whispering river. My anxiety had completely dissipated, making me question how such a thing could have happened. But I didn't ask. What I had was enough.

I ate my dinner and hesitated before calling for the bill. The river had come from the clouds and was continuing its cycle to the sea. Its course would be difficult, with storms, drought, and human pollution, but as it had for eons, the river would continue. And so must I.

That night I sat outside the hotel before heading to bed. There was no breeze, and my mind was as empty and clear as it had been on the veranda. A couple of hotel guests came and went, a little boy was laughing inside, someone had ordered a bottle of rice wine, and at one point I saw the boom-boom lady riding past on her wobbly bike. It was as if I were viewing the entire scene with renewed vision. The world also was continuing on. At that moment, even with its undeniable suffering, this seemed well and good.

The next morning I rose late, packed up, left my backpack behind the front desk, and headed to the monastery. Walking up the stairs to the meditation room, I felt that I was in some sense graduating from this intensive five-day introduction to Buddhism. I took my seat, the monks entered, the bell was rung, we chanted and sat, then the monks filed out. No ceremony, no diploma, just the ongoing routine that was here long before I came and would continue after I had left. That, too, seemed enough.

After pedaling back to the hotel, I dropped off the bike, retrieved my backpack, and headed for the train.

CH 34
MARCH 19, 1996–*Da Nang, Vietnam*

The train was revving its engine as I boarded and took my seat. The compartment was half empty, so I stuffed my backpack into the storage rack and took a window seat, glad to have no one next to me asking me to speak English. Within minutes we had pulled out of Hue, heading for the Hai Van Pass.

The serenity of the night before had waned in the morning's rush, and I was feeling an odd mixture of gratitude, worry, and excitement as I anticipated my homecoming. Trying to relax, I resolved to stay in the moment and enjoy the experience.

There are only two things I remember about the ride to Da Nang. The first was that the pass was as spectacular then as it had been on my first trip through. The one difference was that observing the extensive vistas and treacherous drop-offs through the window wasn't as thrilling as it had been on the back of a screaming motorcycle—but I had no problem with the trade. On the bike my attention had been fixated on the terror of the road, but from the safety of the coach I could fully appreciate the stunning views.

My other memory is of the conversation I had with a young doctor who asked if he could sit next to me and ask a question. He had only one thing on his mind: getting to America. His name was, ironically enough, Hai. He was in his late twenties, of medium build, neatly dressed, and rather intense in his manner. He told me his name in Vietnamese translated as *ocean*, and that was just where he wanted to go: across the sea. Did I have any information how he might do this?

My first thought was that, considering Vietnam's great health needs, it was unfortunate that a qualified doctor intended to leave the country to pursue his fortune in the wealthiest country on earth. I could definitely understand his desire for a freer, more advantaged life, but it still seemed like a loss to his homeland. I asked him about this, but he waved away my concern. "No future here," he stated emphatically. "No way forward." Depending on the criteria, he may have been right about that, but remembering the haggard young doctor at Peace Village, I needed to stifle my judgment so we could have an amiable conversation.

I knew little about immigration, which obviously disappointed my companion. I did say that surely there were agencies, both private and governmental, that might help him with his plan. And how about families of other Vietnamese who had made the transition? He said that he had contacted the agencies and that he had a few connections in American cities that might be helpful. One of them might be able to fix him up with an arranged marriage so he could obtain a green card. At the airport in Taiwan, I'd learned from Major Tony that this was an established method of gaining entrance to the U.S., but I wasn't sure about the requirements involved in acquiring immigrant status in this way.

Hai worked with his father, who was also a doctor, at a clinic in Da Nang, and said he intended to enroll in medical school after he arrived in America so he could become a licensed physician there. It sounded like he definitely had a plan, and I wished him well, thinking our conversation would be over once we rolled into Da Nang. But Hai had become more relaxed as our talk continued, telling me he knew of a decent hotel close to the train station and asking if I'd like to join him for dinner. I said I was grateful for the tip and would be happy to eat with him. After we left the train, it was a two-block walk to the hotel, which was clean and charged only ten dollars for a room. I registered and dropped off my backpack, then we headed downstairs. The restaurant he chose was around the corner, and we settled into a booth next to the front window.

Hai had lots of questions about life in America, and that topic pretty much dominated our conversation. Like most Vietnamese, he wanted to know about social customs, wages, and the price of everything from food to automobiles. We covered several aspects of American life, and he lapped up the information I was giving him, but he couldn't understand how people making middle-wage jobs could still be struggling financially. I told him it had to do with the cost of living, and that in a capitalist country there are many expenses individuals have to pay just to maintain a basic lifestyle. Coming from a world where the average annual wage was a few hundred dollars, he just couldn't get it.

Hai actually became quite animated as we talked, and we started teasing each other about his becoming a famous doctor and my clumsiness with chopsticks (which persisted even after three weeks in an Asian country). He even took to counting my slips when bits of food dropped onto my plate.

"So you'll be chasing nurses around the operating room," I joked.

Hai paused, nodding politely as he stroked his chin. "Four," he said, pointing with his own chopsticks at the noodles hanging off mine. "Maybe you eat better, you get more food to stomach."

Hai was not interested in Tu Hieu or in my fascination with Buddhism. Shrugging away my enthusiasm, he indicated that he had heard of Thich Nhat Hanh but knew little about him. "So many monks," he said, shaking his head. No, his parents were not religious. They observed a few rituals a year, he said, but did not regularly attend a temple or study Buddhist teachings. He went on to say that his friends cared less for the temples than previous generations had. What interested his generation was taking advantage of the new opportunities becoming available with the removal of the trade sanctions.

Hai was very busy organizing his future. "Need to make money," the enterprising young doctor told me. "Plan for trip." I understood his desire for a more advantageous life, but I couldn't help but wonder if this preoccupation with material achievement had undermined the connection to his cultural and spiritual roots, as seemed to be the case in the West.

Hai clearly would have lingered over coffee, but I was done with talking. I told him I had things to do before heading to the airport in the morning and thanked him again. We shook hands on the sidewalk as motorcycles sped by in both directions. Then he went one way and I went another.

While still in Hue, I had had the hotel manager book me a flight from Da Nang to Ho Chi Minh City, so I had a reservation for the next day. Getting that done was bittersweet: mission accomplished—but now the final leg of coming home was imminent. I decided to stroll around the neighborhood surrounding the hotel and continued on for several blocks to decompress from so much gabbing. The city landscape was pretty much what I had seen in Ho Chi Minh City and in Hue: narrow store fronts and small hotels and cafés scattered among commercial establishments (anything from chic women's clothing to second-hand auto parts). The streets hummed with traffic, with motorcycles jetting by in the waning light and the usual assortment of autos, three-wheeled cyclos, and conveyances that defy any name. Pushcarts on wheels, families of four on one bike, and little scooters (some heaped high with produce or stacked lumber) weaved in and out of the automobile and motorcycle traffic.

Passing by the restaurant where we'd eaten, I rounded the corner and came to my hotel. After climbing the stairs, I entered my room and breathed a long sigh of relief to be in my own space. The room was down a long hallway leading toward the back, so the traffic noise was negligible. The room was sparsely furnished with only a bed, a chair, and a small desk, but I was there to sleep and didn't mind the close quarters. The bathroom was to the left of the doorway, and on checking it out, I was surprised to find a full-sized bathtub. The other rooms I'd stayed in had had only showers, which was certainly adequate but lacked the comfort of soaking into a hot, sudsy tub.

Without unpacking, I sat at the desk going over my remaining cash and plane ticket. Since leaving Tu Hieu that afternoon, every step of the way had moved me closer to the point—barely thirty-six hours away—where I'd board the plane back to Taiwan. From there it was a twelve-hour hop to San Francisco. It was a little past eight, and I was feeling a strange mixture of deep fatigue and confused excitement colliding in my body. So much had transpired in the last twenty days, on both an inner and outer level, that my mind felt gridlocked with undigested experience. But as I had the night before, I resolved not to think, opting instead for a hot bath before going to sleep.

I dropped my clothes in the chair and turned on the faucet, anticipating a steady flow of clean water. In other words, I forgot I was in a third-world country. What came out of the tap was certainly steady, and it was water, but the comparison ended there. The liquid pooling in the tub was bright yellow, obviously chemicalized to the hilt to protect bathers from whatever microscopic pathogens lurked in the city's water supply. If I had had to give it a name, I'd have said it was the color of urine. At first I was disgusted, but then I remembered some of the drinking water flown out to us during the war. It was the same color, and here I was twenty-seven years later with no discernable effect. I let the tub fill, and with a shake of my head, climbed in, sank to my chin, closed my eyes, and let the suds work their magic. As long as I didn't think about the chemicals, that was the most comforting bath I remembered having in years.

Ah, Vietnam, I thought. Never a dull moment.

CH 35
MARCH 21, 1996–*Nevada City, California*

The trip home was pretty much a blur. I remember being in the Ho Chi Minh airport but have no memory of the plane ride to Taiwan or negotiating the Taipei airport, and I have only fleeting impressions of the twelve-hour flight to California. I do remember landing in San Francisco around noon and having an hour-long wait for the shuttle bus taking me to my truck in Millbrae. Pulling out of the parking garage, I was glad we'd landed before the rush hour traffic. The road led east, over the Carquinez Strait toward Sacramento, then north into the Sierra Nevada foothills, where the stately oaks started giving way to the towering conifers.

Driving was a thrill after having been carted around for three weeks, and the trip was uneventful, far less stressful than the ride down. Being alone provided a welcome respite after the last couple of days, and I gladly surrendered to the monotonous hum of the truck's engine. After an hour or so, I started playing rock and roll to psyche myself up for my imminent homecoming. Barbara and I had faxed a few times during the journey (email being unavailable to us in 1996), and she filled me in on how our daughter was doing. Claire was thirteen now, entering the forbidding realm of teenage girls, which might not bode well for a smooth reunion.

I contemplated this as I retraced the route home, wondering how our relationship would play out in the years ahead. Since our familial ground was already pretty rocky, the thought of dealing with raging hormones (on top of the vet work) felt like a definite challenge. My primary concern was de-intensifying the family atmosphere, and Tu Hieu had provided the direction for beginning this process. Taking my lessons from the monastery, I was intent on continuing my meditation practice and finding more personal support as I re-entered my life.

"One breath at a time," I kept saying to myself. "One breath at a time."

Reuniting with my family was not the only thing I needed to prepare for. My journey to Vietnam had altered the way I viewed my life in a significant way, but it did not diminish my commitment to the vets. I was bound contractually and ethically to the men I was working with, and I had no intention of abruptly abandoning them. My relationship with several of the guys, who had come into the program only because they knew I was a combat vet and could understand their issues, was crucial to their welfare and that of their families. There was no way I was going to jeopardize their progress.

To do this, it was clear I had to tone down my intensity and change my perspective regarding the vets. Mainly, I needed to let go of the misbegotten belief that by obsessively driving myself in the work I could somehow atone for not being able to save so many of the casualties I had encountered in Vietnam. I thought I could moderate my behavior through daily meditation, getting therapy to deal with the survival guilt, and widening my system of emotional support. At least, that was the plan.

Nearing Nevada City, I realized I wasn't ready to go home yet. My body was aching from the lengthy airplane rides followed by hours in the truck, and I could feel my belly tightening in anticipation of seeing Barbara and Claire. I decided to pull into a graveled parking area just south of town. Walking off the stiffness, I did some deep breathing before climbing back in the truck. My anxiety was escalating, so I leaned back in the seat, and tried to meditate for about twenty minutes. I can't say the sitting calmed me down, but it did ease the tension.

Passing Nevada City, I made the right turn off Highway 49 onto North Bloomfield Road and wound my way two miles up the hill, where a left turn took me the final half mile to the little patio I had left three weeks ago. Thinking about that amazed me—it felt like three months. I parked in front of the house, shut off the engine, and scanned the property that had been my refuge for the last twelve years.

Resting on that familiar ground, I was suddenly overcome with love for Barbara and Claire. Memories of our good years flooded my mind and heart with a gush of warmth I hadn't felt in a long time. I could see us playing games in the yard, laughing as we barbecued on the patio, throwing the ball for Lilly, who chased it with the same exuberance we felt watching her. The desire to see their beloved faces totally outweighed my fear of conflict and rejection, and I harbored a naïve hope that our physical reunion could somehow wipe away the damage done during the previous seven years.

Pulling my backpack from the cab, I approached the house and heard soft music coming through the front door. I stepped inside and saw them at the kitchen table, poring over some papers, probably Claire's schoolwork. Their backs were to me, and I realized they hadn't heard the truck coming up the driveway.

I'd been away for a lot longer than three weeks, lost in a netherworld of my own making, but now I was back. In losing myself in the vet work, I had uprooted myself, lost touch with what was most important in my life. The journey back had restored my footing. Now, absorbed in the vision of my loved ones, I knew exactly where I stood.

I was Home.

EPILOGUE

This is the point where concerned readers would like to hear that the family came together in a huge hug, had a cleansing cry, and began a healing process that restored harmony to our home.

Me too.

But that's not what happened.

When I walked into the kitchen that late Monday afternoon, I reentered the world of family dynamics, teenage angst and veteran therapy. True to form, I'd scheduled myself back to work at 10:00 Wednesday morning—barely forty hours since walking in the door. I was so physically and emotionally drained I could have slept that long, and probably needed a month to chill out and integrate the journey.

The reception I received was fairly tepid. Neither Barbara nor Claire seemed to like the kimonos I had Bac make in Hoi.

And they were bogged down with a school project Claire needed to turn in the next day. I hauled my backpack upstairs, then went outside to throw a ball for Lilly before dinner. We had a low-key meal, and before I knew it, Claire was behind her bedroom door doing whatever young teens do in the sanctuary of their own space.

I was so jetlagged I couldn't sleep for hours. Thrashing around the crumpled sheets, I was utterly exhausted but too wired to relax, let alone sleep. When I woke, Claire had already left for school and Barbara was out doing errands.

That's pretty much how it went going forward. Barbara was busy in her half-time job working with caregivers of the frail elderly, and volunteering at Claire's school. We had a loving reunion along with some deep talks, and I knew she wanted to support me in my reentry. I also knew she was wary of my stress level as I dove back into the PTSD therapy.

For her part, Claire was preoccupied with adjusting to a new school, and had no interest in accommodating the dad she had been alienated from before his trip to Vietnam. In fact, the issue of Vietnam had so inundated her life in the last several years, she was sick of the very word, and wanted nothing do with anything related to that godforsaken country. Or, for that matter, with her beleaguered father.

Scheduling myself back to work so quickly set the tone for how things went. I'd fooled myself in the belief that I could will myself to maintain balance between work and home life, but that illusion was quickly dispelled. Within a week it was clear my depleted nervous system was no match for the heavy stress. Exhausted by the journey, I could barely relate with the vets, and was increasingly irritated by the slightest disruptions at home.

The old pattern was definitely ramping up. I was seeing several vets a day individually, along with the group and backlog of VA paperwork. Coming off the journey, I was emotionally spent at the end of the day and needed space and quiet to rejuvenate. Those are not the likely ingredients of a teenage home, and the normal hubbub of family life increasingly grated on my nerves.

At home, I was keeping my distance to avoid the likelihood of conflict, which pretty much eliminated the possibility of any meaningful contact. As a model of harmonious reconciliation, this arrangement was doomed to fail. Because of our individual differences and needs, my daughter and I were headed for turmoil if something didn't change. But I didn't know what to do.

And then I did.

I had come home with a plan, and realized it was time to implement the insights I'd had at the Tu Hieu monastery. I might not be able to greatly alter my relationship with Claire, but I could change my relationship with myself. Taking the necessary steps, I reentered therapy to face my survivor's guilt, rekindled a few relationships I'd pulled away from, and joined a weekly meditation group. I also started going to meditation retreats through the Community of Mindful Living, Thich Nhat Hanh's North American organization.

Meditation became a daily staple, and I also started looking into Buddhist teachings, finding they related particularly well to how negative mindsets like survivor guilt are formed. It's all in the mind, this ancient religion says.

When a destructive belief (e.g., "I am personally responsible for the deaths of grunts I couldn't save in Vietnam") gets flooded with strong negative emotion, it tends to harden into a rigid conviction defending our position. If left unquestioned, the conviction hardens further into an overriding belief system determining our view of self and the world. The original belief often becomes unconscious, triggering behaviors damaging to the body, mind and personal relationships. Over time, patterns develop that can virtually take over one's identity (e.g., the lone survivor of a firefight becoming a blubbering alcoholic because he sees himself as a coward for not saving his comrades).

The teachings went well with the Cognitive Behavioral Therapy approach the therapist utilized. CBT is a method designed to identify unhealthy beliefs and replace them with ones more realistic and fair to the person (e.g., "I did the best I could in chaotic situations and helped the people I was able to reach").

What it came down to was this: if I believe I'm guilty for not being able to save every wounded soldier in Vietnam, I am casting myself into a combative purgatory from which there's no release. If I am convinced I'm trapped in an inescapable situation, it is that belief, not the setting, that is my jailer.

The bottom line is, I have a choice.

During one session, I remembered my conversation with Jason at the bakery in Hue. The young man had nearly died from his despairing belief that life wasn't worth living without the fiancé who had jilted him. Jason eventually chose life, and I realized that my own predicament was not so different from his. If I couldn't break out of my destructive pattern, long term damage to my health and family was virtually guaranteed.

My therapist made a comment around this time that has stayed with me. "If you refuse to allow yourself a decent life," he said, "aren't you just adding to the carnage?" I saw his point, and decided I was done carrying the baggage of disembodied ghosts.

With the therapist, I devised a ritual in which I called up each wounded Grunt and expressed deep sorrow for his loss and that of his family. I then released him into the arms of Infinity, blessing his journey in whatever form that may take. When the ritual was completed, I still felt deep grief for all the losses, but the guilt was greatly diminished. A deep peace settled over me, and I knew in my heart that I was not to blame for outcomes outside of my control.

Letting go of the guilt was a huge relief. Dealing with Michael's death was a different matter altogether.

There were two issues confronting me about what happened on June 2nd. The first was the trauma of having Michael's face explode in front of mine. I was already reeling from my own wound when he reached me, and had my eyes locked on his as he reached out to switch the field dressing. When the AK-47 round splattered his eye in a crimson gush, Michael's head dropped on the ground less than a foot from my face. We laid there for longer than I can remember, my eyes transfixed on the gaping wound as Michael's breath gurgled through the vomit clogging his throat.

Time passed but the nightmare didn't.

For years, the image of Michael's ruptured blood-splattered eye woke me in the middle of the night, staring at me through the darkness. There was no body or scene, nothing but the dripping red orb jolting me awake. Strangely, the eye would turn into a mouth, a pulsating membrane gyrating wildly in its effort to speak. But it had no lips, no tongue, no vocal capacity whatsoever to form its anguished message. Eventually, its futile effort exhausted, the tortured image would fade, leaving me in a frozen trance and unable to sleep.

It was this trauma, I later realized, that was driving my frenzy in the vet work. The psychological impact had been so great, I would do absolutely anything to keep it from recurring. In the distorted view of Post-Traumatic Stress Disorder, every vet presented a reenactment of that horrific afternoon, and losing even one was a risk I simply could not afford to take.

It took a while, but that insight (along with the ritual mentioned above), enabled me to understand the source of my exaggerated fear. Once my sympathetic system fully realized we were not in combat, and no one's survival was threatened, the overriding urgency eased, and I was able to soften my attitude toward the vets. Working with their issues was still challenging, but it didn't elicit the visceral intensity that had driven me in previous years.

The other issue was far more complicated.

As earlier noted, I'd been acting out some deep shame issues in my gung-ho approach to combat. Having found a "field of dreams" on which I could excel, I stormed into firefights like the white knight I had fantasized myself to be. Big mistake.

On June 2nd I'd continued my foolhardy mission, crawling into the clearing against direct orders and taking the AK-47 round to my chin. Michael followed me into the clearing, and the rest is history. There had always been something simmering below my consciousness about that day. It was years later, at the Tu Hieu monastery, that the realization I'd been avoiding came to me: if I had not crawled into that clearing, Michael probably wouldn't have either.

I couldn't be absolutely sure of that, but it seemed likely. If I hadn't gotten wounded, Michael might not have been sent to the ambush site. But maybe he would have. The CO was sending in reinforcements, so getting another medic close by seems reasonable. Like me, Michael was an intensely altruistic kid, so maybe he would have gone out on his own. That was something I could never know. It was an unanswerable question, and I would have to live with it.

Dealing with the question of my responsibility for Michael's death was one of the hardest things I've had to do. Even though the therapy and rituals helped, I was still left with an emptiness in my heart that I had no idea how to fill.

But now I had a guide.

I'm not remotely qualified to represent the Buddhist way, but I do know how its teachings have affected me since my second Vietnam odyssey. Years of meditation and study helped me see that life itself is an unanswerable question. Dogma aside, we come from the unknown, we go to the unknown, and in the interval dwell in infinite spaciousness beyond human comprehension. Nothing in existence possesses individual nature, our very existence being inextricably interconnected to the entire web of creation. Emptiness is simply the nature of life, and it is our resistance to this basic reality, along with the utter impermanence of life itself, that is the cause of human suffering.

In this way, my spiritual journey now involves learning to cherish the mystery of life rather than trying to explain it through religious doctrine. Accepting the fact that emptiness—like my unanswered question—can never be filled has led me to appreciate existence as an ongoing experiential process shared by all. I am far from embodying this lofty state, but have come to savor the exquisite sweetness of life as expressed in my favorite Buddhist adage: "Not knowing," the saying goes, "is the greatest intimacy." That can be a tough one to grasp, but accepting the unknown would likely ease the tension underlying our conflicts, personal and geopolitical alike.

One thing I greatly valued about Thich Nhat Hanh's approach to Buddhism was his encouragement to not abandon our root religion when exploring the Buddhist way. Whether we are Christian, Jewish or Islamic, for example, he suggested we continue to practice our ancestral religion while incorporating Buddhist teaching into our understanding and behavior. Unless the mind imposes a doctrinal divide, there is no inherent conflict between true religions. Life is a house with many windows, he taught, and every window opens to the same sun. It is essential that we not collapse into dogma that separates us, but expand into the inclusiveness preached by Jesus and the great avatars of all religions.

In this way, I've continued to value Catholicism, seeking to cultivate the "Christ Consciousness" at the core of all spirituality.

There was still the issue of the nightmare. The "visitation," as I called it, occurred several times a year, most often near our June 2nd anniversary date. I never understood the dream's meaning, or what Michael was trying to communicate. But in 2003, when George Bush bombed Baghdad against international opposition, I found a way to give my friend his voice.

Outraged by the wanton killing of civilians, I wrote a news article titled "The Michael MacParlane Taste Test." Describing Michael's wound in graphic detail, I related how, on the bullet's impact, Michael's body fluids squirted into my mangled mouth. If you haven't taken this test, I said, don't even think about sending our kids into combat because you don't know what war is. There was no doubt in my mind that Michael would have approved of his story being used to challenge the slaughter of innocent civilians.

I sold the essay to the *San Francisco Chronicle* and the *Common Ground Journal* in the Bay Area. Getting the essay published was satisfying, but what came out of the experience was way more important. A few months after the essay was published, I received a call from a woman who said she was Michael's niece. She told me that her mother, Michael's only sibling, was bedridden with a terminal illness in Tucson, Arizona, and would love to hear from me. I was flabbergasted, but delighted by the news and eager to make the connection.

And this began my three-year relationship with Eileen Meade, a friendship that enriched both our lives.

We rarely talked, but exchanged two or three emails a week. Sharing our histories and current situations, we came to know one another more intimately than people we'd known all our lives. She told me all about Michael's childhood, how his parents had been crushed by his death, and how sad she still was about losing her little brother.

Eileen also talked freely about her impending death, saying she looked forward to "getting my wings." She was a person of great faith despite not being affiliated with any religion, and saw life as simply a spiritual adventure in a human body. If she had a motto, it would have been something like, "I'm game for whatever comes, so bring it on." I admired her courage more than I can say.

It was my privilege to help Eileen deal with her physical pain and deep grief about earlier experiences in her life. She was more a giver than a taker, and wasn't used to being deeply heard, but I drew her out on the lingering sorrow regarding her childhood and failed marriage. Over time, Eileen was able to open up about her disappointments and, a month before the disease took her, she told me our discussions helped prepare her for death.

Eileen often spoke about how much she loved her children. For her, family was a God-given gift that made life worth living, and she wanted to cherish every possible moment with them before her body succumbed to the illness. She became a fierce advocate for me to prioritize my life regarding work and family. "You have a job that's going to end at some point," she often told me, "and a daughter who will be with you for life. Make sure you know which one is most important."

I continued working with vets for seven more years, gradually shifting most of the work to subcontractors. The changes I made did not bring immediate relief, but with continued practice (on and off the cushion), I continued softening my reactivity, and maintained a more loving presence at home. There were still upsets, but love prevailed, and our disagreements were increasingly handled in a way that preserved family harmony.

After high school, Claire earned a degree in Theater Arts at Santa Clara University. Having witnessed how Buddhism helped me, she attended a three-month meditation retreat in the Bay Area before moving to New York City. She worked in her field for seven years before returning to California to get a Master's Degree, then taught for several years in Los Angeles, and now lives in San Francisco where she is developing a theater arts program at a local school. We are delighted to have her closer, and spend as much time together as her busy schedule allows. I love and admire my daughter more than I can say.

Years later, Claire presented me with a Father's Day present I'll always treasure. On the face of a small locket, she had two circles engraved, a smaller one within the protective ring of the larger. The symbol said everything I needed to hear about the restoration of our relationship. We still had our issues, and I continue learning how to be softer and less reactive in our interactions.

Barbara and I just passed our forty-ninth anniversary, and remain deeply committed to our love and support for one another as we go through our senior years. In 2019 we moved to a co-housing community on the edge of Nevada City. Our homeowners association is composed of thirty-four privately owned homes on eleven acres. We work collectively to maintain the property, upgrade our facilities and enhance group cohesion.

Living in community supports the interconnectedness we value in a world that seems increasingly addicted to warfare and environmental self-destruction. My hope is that this small book may encourage readers toward greater love for themselves, their families, our global neighbors and this beautifully alive world we are so privileged to inhabit.

Acknowledgments

If it takes a village to raise a child, it takes a community to produce a book. In the years compiling this manuscript, I have been blessed with a number of folks who have supported and guided me throughout the writing process.

Beyond all else, I bow in gratitude to my partner Barbara Larsen. Her steadfast support over the years of reading drafts, making suggestions, and providing heartfelt support when I floundered are appreciated beyond measure.

Special thanks to my book designer, Patricia Arnold of Menagerie Design & Publishing. Patricia's courage and dedication to this project, while dealing with serious health issues, rank her as a true warrior, both personally and professionally. My gratitude and respect for her runs deep.

In the earlier days, the late Jim Kavenaugh drove me to complete my first Vietnam manuscript, and later called his publisher, Random House, in front of me to arrange a reading. Jim's confidence in my writing was invaluable to my learning and confidence as a budding artist.

Special thanks to my dear friend and sister, Joanna Phillips, for her literary and emotional support throughout the journey. Special thanks also to the esteemed author, Maxine Hong Kingston, the godmother of veteran writing. Over the years, Maxine's inspiration, encouragement and guidance have enabled innumerable veterans to tell their stories.

To the other word pros who have contributed their expertise and inspiration along the way, I give thanks to: Donna Hanelin, Judy Crowe, Judy Rae, Maxima Kahn, Jordan Fisher Smith, Jeff Kane, Gail and Charles Entrekin, Elle Gianforte, Richard Frishman and Michael Cohen.

I also thank my neighbors and friends, Ben Levy and Theo Fitanides, for their skill and willingness to keep my computer operating despite my continuous abuse of that miraculous machine.

Last, but far from least, I am truly indebted to Kit Bailey, the remarkable copy editor and new friend who guided me through the process of getting this book ready to publish.

BIO

William Larsen is a disabled Vietnam veteran who has worked for fifty-two years as a psychotherapist specializing in trauma recovery. He served as a contract psychotherapist with the Veterans Administration for fourteen years, treating traumatized veterans suffering from PTSD symptoms similar to his own. In 1996, William returned to Vietnam on a healing journey that introduced him to Buddhism and a new way of viewing traumatic loss. He is a contributor to the book *Veterans of War, Veterans of Peace*, edited by Maxine Hong Kingston, and will be included in a sequel to this work coming out in the near future. William is the proud father of Claire Larsen, and lives with his wife Barbara in Nevada City, California.